Fifty Years of Counselling: My Presenting Past

Fifty Years of Counselling: My Presenting Past

Michael Jacobs

 Open University Press

Open University Press
McGraw-Hill Education
8th Floor, 338 Euston Road
London
England
NW1 3BH

email: enquiries@openup.co.uk
world wide web: www.openup.co.uk

and Two Penn Plaza, New York, NY 10121-2289, USA

First published 2018

A catalogue record of this book is available from the British Library

ISBN-13: 978-0-335-22710-5
ISBN-10: 0-33-522710-4
eISBN: 978-0-335-22711-2

Library of Congress Cataloging-in-Publication Data
CIP data applied for

Typeset by Transforma Pvt. Ltd., Chennai, India
Printed and bound in Great Britain by Bell and Bain Ltd, Glasgow

Fictitious names of companies, products, people, characters and/or
data that may be used herein (in case studies or in examples) are not
intended to represent any real individual, company, product or event.

Praise for this book

"A delight to read! Everyone benefits from a lovely memoir like this: students, experienced colleagues, and the author himself. Michael has built a deserved reputation as an outstanding authority and innovator in the counselling field, in practice as well as in training. His restlessness and his challenging nature are still needed as the sense of crisis in depth and relational therapy work intensifies. The account of his experiences, whether entirely fortuitous and haphazard or fuelled by an individuating sense of vocation, will stimulate thought, feeling and a profound questioning of where our field is heading."

Professor Andrew Samuels, Department
of Psychosocial and Psychoanalytic
Studies, University of Essex, UK

"This is the moving and revelatory account of the personal and professional evolution of one of Britain's most prominent pioneering counsellors. In telling his own story, Michael Jacobs also illuminates the development of the counselling movement during the past fifty years and younger readers will discover much to inform and surprise them.

It is doubtful that such an intrepid pioneer could survive let alone flourish in today's highly regulated therapeutic culture. Jacobs' book is a stirring reminder of an exciting and creative past and a grim warning of the risk-averse future that may lie ahead. His life demonstrates both the cost and the rewards of embracing vulnerability and of taking on the power of institutions. This deceptively passionate book inspires and challenges on almost every beautifully written page."

"Michael Jacobs's new memoir kept me wide-awake for most of the night, because I simply could not put this book down! Written with consummate story-telling skills, Jacobs has created an inspiring and enthralling portrait of his remarkable career in the fields of psychotherapy and counselling. A true pioneer of mental health in Great Britain, Jacobs has much to teach us all, and I recommend this new volume most heartily!"

"At a time when BACP shows its disrespect for those senior figures who contributed to its development by requiring them to take the counselling equivalent of the cycling proficiency test to remain a member, along comes this wonderful, gem of a book written by one of British counselling's elder statesman. Michael Jacobs has made many fine contributions to the field, many detailed here, and in his own engaging writing style, he has also given a personal view on how counselling has developed since the early pioneering days. This book should be read by all those who train counsellors and who work in student counselling. Wise words from a wise man".

From Freud's letter to his nephew Edward Bernays when he suggested a biography of Freud:

A psychologically complete and honest confession of life ... would require so much indiscretion ... about family, friends and enemies, most of them still alive, that it is simply out of the question. What makes all autobiographies worthless is, after all, their mendacity.

(E. Freud, 1970: 390–1)

Contents

Preface

There have, of course, been more than fifty years of counselling. Under different names counsel has taken place since time immemorial in all cultures between two or more people, one of whom has often been particularly sensitive to the issues of living and dying. Even the more modern use of the term 'counselling' has been used of a particular style of helping relationship long before my own involvement in the discipline. I refer in later chapters to something of that history.

But my own career as a therapist started fifty years ago around the time when counselling in Britain was becoming distinguished from psychoanalysis and psychotherapy, from psychological interventions, from guidance and advice. As I took my first tentative steps in the discipline, those who were trained as counsellors were beginning to form national associations, develop trainings and publish British books on the subject. I have been privileged to be one of the pioneers of developments in training, in the literature and in the institutionalisation of the twin disciplines of counselling and psychotherapy.

As yet, no one has written a comprehensive history of this movement, which has gone from those relatively small beginnings to become, in some ways regrettably, such an industry. Regrettably, because my story tells how a number of us, with differing degrees of training and experience, learned on the hoof, and forged careers that would, at least in my own case, be impossible to get into now without having had to spend a lot of money (which I did not have) and time qualifying for a career; so it sometimes seems that professionalisation and bureaucracy have replaced creative learning and service.

This book is about my experience over fifty years. I have been fortunate in having had many people who have spotted my potential and have supported me in many ways, not only through the developments in counselling and psychotherapy in general, but specifically in my own progress. Many have given me openings and opportunities that I have seized upon and which I hope I have done justice to. Some of them have since died, and others I may have lost touch with over the years. All of them, and no doubt many others with whom I have worked as a colleague and as a therapist, have in one way or another contributed at different times to the professional life that I record in these pages: Derek Blows, Hugh Clegg, Jimmy Crighton, John and Marcia Davis, Windy Dryden, Jacinta Evans, Edward Finch, Bill Forster, Richard Herrick, Kenneth Horner, Pam Howdle-Smith, Isobel Hunter-Brown, Valerie Jacobs, Daniel Jenkins, David Johnson, Cheslyn Jones, Eric Kemp, Frank Lake, Monika Lee, Peter Lomas, Judith Longman, David Lyall, Kathryn Noble, Simon Phipps, Eric Rayner, Denis Rice, Lesley Riddle, Anthony Ryle, Doreen Schofield, John Skelton, Robin Skynner, Mary Swainson, John Todd, David Toms, Leslie Virgo, Moira Walker, Pippa Weisz, Mary Welch, Colin Whurr, Ernie Williams, Susan Worsey, Derek Wright.

Michael Jacobs
Swanage, June 2017

1

An accidental beginning

I never intended to become a therapist. If it had not been for my ineptitude at Greek and my weak Latin, it might never have happened.

I was reading theology at Oxford. Back then any Arts subject required some Latin and sometimes another language – Anglo-Saxon for English, New Testament Greek for theology. My degree also included a compulsory special subject, and all those that attracted me (philosophy of religion, psychology of religion) similarly required the study of texts in these ancient languages. Put off by my inability to read such texts without constant recourse to a dictionary, I considered a rarely used option – a *special* special subject, which had to be approved by the examiners.

This may seem a long way from psychotherapy and counselling, and indeed it was – ten years in fact before I became a university counsellor. But its relevance, like so much in therapy, will become obvious in time. I thought up a subject, one which interested me but which I knew little about, and which (so I thought) would enable me to avoid having to study Latin and Greek texts. The special subject I proposed was mysticism. I had read biographies of Teresa of Avila and John of the Cross, and had come across English mystics such as Dame Julian of Norwich and Richard Rolle, as well as the anonymous *The Cloud of Unknowing*. I thought that I could study those as set texts in English, since as a theology undergraduate I would not be required to have Spanish or mediaeval English as additional languages.

But Oxford would not let me get away so easily with such devious avoidance of the classical texts. My submission was approved, and the Spanish and English mystics' texts I proposed were accepted, but the examination board insisted I also study Clement of Alexandria (in Greek) and someone else whom I forget (in Latin). Hoist by my own petard!

My special subject indeed proved to be interesting, and I lost myself in the mystical language – this was the start of the 1960s. Not that Clement or the Latin author fired me up, but otherwise I got the bug and wanted to take my studies further. With a decent degree, and two years ahead of me at theological college, I set my sights on a postgraduate degree. Since my degree meant that I was what is now called APEL'd for many of the subjects taught at theological college, I would only need to study for one year to complete my professional exams. So I would research Margery Kempe – that strange mad mystic – in my second year while I waited for ordination.

Whether or not my college principal was right, he refused to let me follow my plan. Yet again I was frustrated. Being a priest, he claimed with some justification, required the ability to switch easily between tasks. Such research was like knitting, which could be taken up in spare moments between other duties. (He was fond of domestic imagery, cooking being another.) Therefore I must spread out my remaining exams over the two years, and I could then pick up Margery Kempe in the spaces between.

While he was right about the life of a priest, he did not know me. If I want to achieve an object, I prefer to go hammer and tongs at it until it is completed or I give up on it altogether. (This trait, which is a strength as well as a weakness, will become apparent in later chapters.) So the 'knitting' that I took up between lectures and writing essays on the few subjects I still had to study consisted not of research but more of making two model galleons, which graced my home for many years. Margery Kempe went into abeyance and never emerged again, although she had still helped me on my way.

I completed my two years at theological college and went to a parish in Walthamstow as an assistant curate, learning on the stump about pastoral care. Believe it or not my training at theological college had in no way prepared me for relating to distressed people, or for the variety of issues arising in their lives. At college I had had a placement in a local mental hospital, where we were encouraged to talk with the in-patients, but if there was any preparatory instruction for that task I cannot remember it. What I do remember is overhearing a fellow student talking to an elderly woman who was sat knitting. As her needles clicked away – as I gather Anna Freud's did in analysis (Couch, 1995) – my friend asked her what she did all day. 'I knit and knit and knit,' she replied, to which this aspiring priest responded, 'Goodness me, that would drive me mad!'

It was July 1965. I had only been in the parish four weeks, and had just returned with my wife Valerie from a week's totally exhausting 'holiday' with ten boisterous ten-year-old children of parishioners, when the doorbell rang. 'Answer that, could you?' I asked irritatingly, but Valerie soon called me to the front door. 'It's the police. They want you,' she said. And so began my first serious therapeutic encounter – with Harry from over the road. He had returned from his retirement party at work with the obligatory clock to find that his wife had gassed herself in the kitchen. Entering the still gas-filled hallway and finding the dazed old man in his front room, I had to draw upon my non-existent pastoral skills.

I need not go into any detail about Harry, who might in one way be called my first client. He attached himself to me, and I learned the hard way about boundaries. He started to come to church for the first time, and transferred his attachment to two older single women who took him under their wing. He still kept me informed of what was happening to him, even after he met someone from the West Country on a train, rapidly married her, and moved to her hometown. He wrote and told me with great pride that he had been made a churchwarden in the local church. A successful piece of pastoral care? Who knows, but if it was it was more by luck than judgement. I often think of him as I think we do of our very first clients.

There was in fact training in pastoral counselling at that time, although not all immediately available to me. What would have been the more relevant training was not deemed suitable for a new curate. I would need to wait three years before I would be permitted to join the local Clinical Theology group to which my vicar belonged. This was a form of pastoral counselling developed by Frank Lake, a psychiatrist who had returned from mission work in India. He had begun teaching seminars in clinical theology in 1958 and founded the Clinical Theology Association in 1962. Many groups in different localities had been formed, mainly of clergy, to study his work. His tome *Clinical Theology* was published in 1966. His work partly kick-started pastoral counselling in England, and at the time influenced a considerable number of clergy. He will figure again in a later chapter, but as far as I was concerned at the time, Clinical Theology represented a secret society that I was not yet permitted to join, and in the end never did join, even though I had much to do with it in different capacities when I became a therapist.

Clinical Theology would have remained a completely arcane area for me had it not been for a registrar in psychiatry at a local mental hospital, one of my own age, who was a member of the congregation. We were at much the same stage of our respective careers, with a first child of the same age. David Toms knew about Clinical Theology and he lent me photostat copies of Lake's commentaries on certain New Testament figures, who were exemplars that Lake had developed of different diagnostic categories taken from psychoanalysis, such as the hysteric (Mary Magdalene), the obsessional, the phobic person, etc. I was impressed by Lake's exposition of the New Testament texts, and fascinated by the way he tied this in to what I vaguely knew about psychiatric disorders.

I was however allowed to undertake another training option in group relations. This was the flavour of the month in the diocese of Chelmsford where I was working, a Tavistock Institute of Human Relations style of group dynamics, adapted from the Leicester conferences, which I was later to encounter in various ways when I worked at the University of Leicester. The intention of Richard Herrick, the diocese training officer, was to provide a training in how groups functioned, since they were an inevitable feature of any organisation, including church parochial councils, congregations, and so on.

This was my first ever taste of experiential learning. Group relations training involved a couple of five-day residential conferences in Clacton-on-Sea, with the majority of sessions consisting of small groups with two consultants in each, studying the 'here-and-now'. The approach, for those unfamiliar with it, can be illustrated by what happened at my first session on the first day of my first residential conference. My wife's grandfather had died, and I was to officiate at the funeral in Sussex the very day the training started. Having agreed with the course director that I could arrive late, I missed the introductory plenary session where the purpose of the week had been explained (which to this day I do not know). I arrived at the hotel after the first small group session had started. There was no one around to register my arrival, but I found a noticeboard that told me which group and which room I was in. They had been meeting already for about half the ninety-minute session.

I found the door to the room, knocked and went straight in. There was one vacant chair in the circle of group members, which I assumed was for me. I sat down, looked around the group, and they looked at me. No one spoke. Imagining that I had interrupted what I thought was the flow of conversation, I assumed a low profile and waited to hear what they had been talking about. After a few minutes more silence during which I felt embarrassed at having broken into the group discussion, I decided to speak. 'I suppose I had better introduce myself. My name is Michael Jacobs and I have had to take a funeral of a relative today which is I why I am late. I don't know what you have been talking about.' There was a tangible air of relief in the room. 'Well,' said one of the others, 'You're the first person to speak!' They then for the first time introduced themselves to me and to each other.

The two consultants had clearly said nothing, and when they later spoke they uttered totally esoteric sentences, such as, 'I think there's going to be an execution before long', 'Perhaps we should prepare a grave'. So profound and obscure were their interventions that such are the only words from them that stick in my memory, and even then I cannot be sure I heard them right. We thought that over the course of the conference we had completely sussed our two consultants. One was a good guy, whom we liked, the other a bad guy, whom we hated; and we thought that was indeed the way they were as persons. Only after attending the second training residential did we realise, talking to members of another group, who now had the same two consultants, that their perceptions were completely opposite to our own! The one we hated they liked; the one we liked they hated. That was when I first learned about splitting.

I also learned that having been the one to break the long silence, that was what was expected of me from then on.

I had assumed a group role, which I might describe as an initiator. It may of course have been pure coincidence, but that role has continued to be typical of my career, taking a lead, suggesting new projects, initiating ideas that are often taken up with enthusiasm by others, while I often moved on to the next possibility. Many years later I was told by one of the key figures in the development of counselling, Francesca Inskipp, that her husband John had been a member of that first group and had confided to her that I had indeed taken up such a position in the training group.

Having attended my first group dynamics training, I found I had joined an elite group of those who had themselves at one time been through the experience, and when meeting each other would talk the same kind of language that the consultants had used. Anyone listening to such conversations who had not attended such a group would fail to understand what we were talking about, which of course made us feel superior as if we were on another level of psychological understanding. We had been initiated into a cult, and yearned to become consultants.

I was later to become a consultant of sorts myself at Parish Life Conferences in the diocese of Chichester, when I was working at the University of Sussex. They were designed to encourage teams of lay men and women from parishes to look at what their church was doing, and inspire them to engage in different types of action. On those occasions there were sessions that had clear objectives and encouraged focused discussion. But there was also one session on the last evening that was run as an unstructured group. Unstructured except that the brief was for the consultant team to observe the dynamics as the group members became more and more lost in what they were meant to be doing. One of the team was briefed to act the bad guy, making these obscure interventions. This was I think a travesty of group relations training, since in our own training those good/bad roles came from the group (I still assume!) and not from any planning. The session sent people off to bed frustrated and hopping mad, but the next morning they were determined to show us that they were going to channel all that negative energy into positive ends. I came to see it as a very manipulative strategy on the part of the consultants. The theory seemed to owe something to a rather dubious feature of some psychoanalytic practice, that in allowing silence, the consequent frustration promotes feelings, insight and learning.

I later learned not to allow my prejudices and projections to be the only version of the truth. I had found the residential course director, Richard Herrick, cold and severe and felt in awe of him. Many years later in Leicester I gathered that while he was a consultant at one of the Leicester/Tavistock conferences he had had a heart attack, and was in a Leicester hospital. I knew I should visit him, and approached the task with some foreboding. My fears and apprehension were needless, since he was human after all, and we got on well. But I was never to see him again.

I come to early 1967, when I had been in the parish two years and had told my vicar, Edward Finch, that I wanted to serve another two years before moving on. Then, not quite out of the blue, a letter came from my Oxford college chaplain, Eric Kemp. I had the previous year been asked to preach at the Commemoration of Benefactors, and perhaps that had been a trial run for his present request. He was due to take a term's sabbatical at the end of the year, and invited me to be the locum chaplain for three months. The college was prepared to accommodate my family (now with one daughter and a baby on the way) and my duties were mainly to conduct the daily services. It would give me plenty of time to study for my research into Margery Kempe.

Eric was a quiet man, a good listener, and underneath his shy exterior a warm-hearted person. He was a powerful influence in the Church of England, the only real expert on the revision of canon law – the laws that govern the church. He invited Valerie and myself to his home for a few days to prepare for my sabbatical from parish work, and I remember him taking us for a meal in Abingdon where he hoped we might not bump into the retired Archbishop of Canterbury, Geoffrey Fisher, who must have lived nearby. I gathered that the archbishop was in Eric's word 'mad' – the first insight he had let me have into the Church in which I had chosen to pursue my career. 'Dementia' would have been a kinder description.

I explained to Eric that I wanted to spend my time in Oxford preparing the ground for my research into Margery Kempe. I have sometimes thought that Eric saw me at the time, young though I was, as destined for office in the church, and was helping me prepare the way. But his advice for my time in Oxford is probably responsible for a career change he could not have envisaged, and perhaps even regretted. I could not possibly research Margery Kempe, he wisely said, without a grounding in psychology, for Margery, perhaps like Geoffrey Fisher, showed signs of madness – although with hindsight I imagine that hers was a sign of psychosis. I should, on my arrival in Oxford, visit Roy Lee, vicar of the University Church and chaplain at Nuffield College, for advice on my reading.

And that was the turning point. I had up to that time been reading Jung, which, in line with my interest in mysticism, had kept me in line with my theology and my slender spirituality: Jung may not have been at all an orthodox Christian, but he had been made so by many in the church who wanted to integrate psychology with their faith. He remains such a figure for those who wish to develop their spirituality, seen for example in the interest in Myers-Briggs, developed from Jungian typology. I was fast becoming a devotee and had in my first week picked up a number of second-hand copies of Jung's *Collected Works* in Blackwell's. But Roy Lee soon disabused me. 'Read Freud,' he said, 'he is more scientific.' Lee had recently published *Freud and Christianity* (1967) in Britain, which he obviously recommended, and was later to write *Principles of Pastoral Counselling* (1973), which my first book fifteen years later was intended to replace. He also suggested that I attend his lectures that term, which were delivered mainly for those training for the church in Oxford theological colleges. I did all he recommended: I read his book, I bought books by Freud and on Freud, and I went to his lectures. I was trapped. Freud became my new saint. Margery Kempe was once again put to one side, and she has never reared her head since (except for MacDonald, 2014).

It was an enthralling time. Apart from Oxford itself, this time as a member of the Senior Common Room, I knew that I wanted to work in a university, even though I did not have a postgraduate degree (which in those days was not uncommon); and I wanted to absorb as much of Freud as I could. I returned to Walthamstow as a convert, and was immediately contributing to my vicar's lay training programme on the significance of Freud for pastoral work, arrogantly thinking I knew it all. I was also determined to end my planned four-year stay in Walthamstow a year early in order to secure an academic post. I got nowhere with my first application, setting my sights low on the post of chaplain at a Church of England teacher training college. I was one of a dozen short-listed candidates. At my second attempt, for the post of interdenominational chaplain at the University of Sussex, where I was one of two short-listed candidates, I was offered the job. Fortune had shone upon me. I was, unknown to me, on the next and crucial step towards my eventual career and towards the opportunity to be one of the pioneers in the development of counselling.

2

Changes of direction

The place: Brighton and the University of Sussex. The date: 1968. Myself aged 27, just a few years older than the student population. Sussex was one of a wave of new universities built in the 1960s, and together with Essex and Warwick and the somewhat older LSE, it was at that time at the forefront of the movement for student power in Britain. It was perhaps that ferment of ideas that had put others off applying for the post of chaplain, making for an easier ride for me: and certainly I was asked at my interview whether I thought what was going on in Paris, where students were occupying the universities and the streets, would come over here. I thought not. I was half right, but also half wrong.

I was to be junior chaplain to Dr Daniel Jenkins, a generation older than me, and as much an academic as the senior chaplain. I, as the younger man, was to mix with the students, to engage with them in their student life, to debate with them in their thinking, to be alongside them in their issues. I had to find a role in a setting that was far removed from a conventional Church of England parish. Responsibility for conducting services was minimal, even if important. I was working at a time when the question was being asked, 'What is a university?', a question which might well be debated again in our present day, since universities have changed in my lifetime from places of access to learning and questioning to production lines for qualifications. The years 1968/70 in particular were challenging times as I looked around for opportunities to exercise a different kind of ministry.

There was no counselling service at Sussex – and indeed any such service was rare in most other universities. Leicester had had one since 1948, Keele since the mid-1960s; Cambridge was to open a Counselling Medical Service in 1969, while Oxford watched developments there and opened a similar service in 1972 (Walker, 1979). I certainly had no concept of anything such as that beforehand. Sussex, like most other British universities, had a student health service – the British Student Health Association had been formed in 1951. The director of the Sussex service, Dr Tony Ryle, would later develop cognitive-analytic therapy (CAT). I soon learned the service's reputation from the students I mixed with: that if you went there with a sports injury, you would soon find yourself on the couch – that is, the analyst's couch. It was an exaggeration, to be sure, but the doctors (and one nurse and a researcher) were themselves in therapy, and they practised more psychotherapy with that healthy age group than they did general medicine. Nevertheless, their service was well used. Tony Ryle had a reputation amongst his colleagues, I later learned, for really long-term work, which may seem strange when CAT is usually limited to sixteen sessions, but that is another story.

Given my interest in Freud, it was not long before I decided to make contact with Tony Ryle, wondering rather precociously whether we might work cooperatively. I really do not know what I had in mind except misplaced confidence. However, Tony met me for a lunchtime drink, and he was very welcoming. He seemed interested and suggested their consultant psychotherapist, Isca Salzberger-Wittenberg, a Kleinian psychoanalyst and author (1970), interview me. Needless to say, I knew nothing about Klein at this point.

A time was arranged when she was visiting from London. I remember nothing of the interview, except feeling overwhelmed at the thought of being psychoanalysed by an authoritative *woman*, a leading light in the field of psychoanalysis. Up to that time – at school, in my Oxford College, and in the Church – it had been men who had been the authority figures. Not surprisingly, I was really unsure of myself.

I heard no more: nothing from her, nothing from Tony Ryle. My initiative had sunk without trace. It was to be expected considering what a novice I was, having read a little, but knowing nothing from experience about the field. But not hearing was ignominious. I clearly was not acceptable. I needed to look elsewhere for a role.

Though I continued to read Freud – and other books on psychoanalysis – counselling was not what I first had in mind. The intellectual ferment at Sussex engaged me, and got me thinking in a different way from my Oxford education. It was impossible not to be drawn into the student milieu, to take part in the sit-ins, to be engaged in a constant debate about educational issues as well as national and international politics. I mixed with Maoists, Marxists, Trotskyists, without knowing the differences between them, but was carried along on a wave of radicalism. I remember preaching in a Sussex public school on 'the guerrilla church', drawing lessons for the Church from my reading about Che Guevara. Many students in the interdenominational Christian community had similar concerns, as they hammered out theological questions and the relationship of those questions to political issues. The progressive interdenominational Christian community (distinct from the fundamentalist Christian Union) led the way with hunger lunches, and such activities as the screening in the university of Martin Cole's controversial *Growing Up*, an explicit educational sex film. I took my bank account away from Barclays because of their overseas activities in South Africa, and invited the Managing Director of their overseas operations to speak to the student body. He accepted and debated the issue. As a member of a team of chaplains representing the different churches, some full-time, some part-time, I valued the ecumenical spirit of the time, at one time becoming President of the Catholic Society, and being taken by them to Rome for the canonisation of the English Martyrs. They were remarkably exciting times, giving me opportunities to live the life of a student, to attend lectures and seminars, without having to write essays or sit exams. This breadth of involvement in such different activities was to go on influencing me as I moved into a very different role as a therapist, but it also made that move harder, as I shall show, as I shifted from a somewhat manic existence to a more depressive one.

What I knew at the time was that there was no way I could have moved from that freedom back into parochial ministry, where change seems to move like a convoy at the pace of the slowest. My theology too was under the microscope. Daniel Jenkins preached a modern theology, to which I had never been exposed in a traditional Oxford theology degree and a conservative Anglo-Catholic theological college. As it should be in a university context, my own sermons addressed my own questioning. The Freudian (and some Jungian) influence was still making an impact on me, although it was my Marxist leanings that figured rather more strongly in my first two years at Sussex. And it might have remained so had it not been for the arrival of a young man, about my age, a Cambridge graduate, who was to work in the student health service as a non-medical psychotherapist.

Hugh Clegg had just completed postgraduate psychotherapy training at the University of Aberdeen. He was keen to become involved in the activities of the chaplaincy, and he and I hit it off from the start. My interest in Freud was now given an extra dimension since Hugh, so recently qualified and I suspect eager to show what he knew, found me a very eager pupil. I was not at that point engaged in much one-to-one pastoral care such as a priest might offer, but Hugh encouraged me to begin seeing people for therapy. Looking back, what a suggestion! I knew from my reading (or I thought I knew) what was involved, how I should conduct sessions. He wanted to supervise my practice. I knew about boundaries – although I was inevitably going to be confusing them when my 'clients' were also members of the worshipping community. I knew I had to make it clear that there was to be no socialising with clients as there might be with other students and staff, only gradually learning that my presence at worship, dressed in vestments and speaking about various matters in my sermons, was bound to affect 'the transference'.

Remarkably, it worked. I think I did some good. I probably made mistakes, and no doubt at times I made interpretations that were as beyond me as they were beyond my clients. But my week slowly came to include five to six hours of counselling of both staff and students, and I learned a huge amount as I went along. Hugh supervised my work once or twice a week, although he was probably as green a supervisor as I was a therapist. I had also begun to do a little extra-mural teaching, and we planned and taught a course on various aspects of human relations the following year.

I am not sure I am recommending starting in this way, although it will become clear that I am also critical of the over-stringent requirements that are now in place for those who practise as counsellors. I was learning on the job, and I seized the opportunity, on Hugh's suggestion, that I try once more to liaise with the student health service. I arranged for a second time to meet with Tony Ryle, who it seemed had forgotten that I had ever been vetted by Isca Salzberger-Wittenberg, saying he had heard nothing more from her. We would start again, but this time I would be interviewed by their new consultant, Dr Fred Shadforth, another Kleinian psychoanalyst practising in Hove. This time I was accepted. I must have learned something.

There was however a problem. There was shared confidentiality within the health service team, and I would be a visitor, not a colleague, so there was no way that confidential information could be shared with me. I could therefore attend their theoretical seminars, which were held weekly, when they discussed articles in psychoanalytic journals, but I could not attend their weekly case seminars. This arrangement soon broke down when I pointed out, having been accepted into the seminar group, that the others were illustrating their theoretical observations with cases of patients they were currently seeing. If I was party to that information there, what then was the problem about attending case seminars as well? By that time I had earned sufficient confidence from the team and there was no difficulty deciding I should be admitted to those seminars as well. Twice weekly seminars, theoretical and practical: it is not surprising that I learned so much over those eighteen months.

What I was eagerly absorbing about therapy was simultaneously challenging beliefs that I had already been questioning deeply. Tony Ryle was keen on research and, as part of the assessment of his patients, he was using the repertory grid, a tool developed by George Kelly and based on the theory of personal constructs. It has been well explained by Fay Fransella, who would later contribute to one of the books in my series *In Search of a Therapist* (1996a; see also her book *Personal Construct Counselling in Action*, co-authored with Peggy Dalton, 1990). Tony was through and through a psychoanalytic psychotherapist, but his use of a psychometric tool from another modality pre-figured his design of the tests he developed for use in cognitive-analytic therapy. The repertory grid consisted of comparing numerically the constructs (which might very loosely be translated as 'perceptions') that we have of key figures in our lives, and (because it was a two-way type of repertory grid) our perceptions of how they see us.

I never used the test myself in my work at the time, nor have I ever used any tests in my later work. I can see the value of such tools, particularly those such as the CORE (Clinical Outcomes in Routine Evaluation) model for assessment and outcome research, which can also be used as an aid in funding applications to show the effectiveness of services. But I was interested in undertaking the repertory grid for myself, and Tony Ryle took me through it. The first results were hopeless. I had idealised my relationships and found it difficult to admit to negative feelings. Such was my naïve personal awareness. We agreed I should take it again, and this time I was more in touch with what I actually felt about my parents, my wife, my children, and (in my case) significant figures like God and Christ. I was surprised by the results, identifying how I perceived the 'mythical' figures as idealised parental introjects. I wanted to see whether other Christians might show similar results, so I secured cooperation from my old theological college principal to approach a number of his students to take the test. I do not pretend to understand the finer points of the repertory grid, but what seemed patent to me was that their images of God had the same qualities as mine, that they related to God and believed God related to them in the same way as their imagined ideal mother. This was the God I and they called God the Father.

I recount this episode to show how intellectually I was moving away from the orthodox position I had held for many years, under the influence first of Freud, then Marx, as well as my exposure to modern theology – these were also the years of the *Honest to God* debate. Intellectually I was enormously stimulated. Emotionally, too. I was no longer satisfied by my beliefs. At the same time I was experiencing a more profound relationship with those who came to me to talk, and amateur though I was, I was realising that I could offer more through my counselling practice to those in crisis, and to a wider spectrum of people including those outside the Church, than I could through the rudimentary spiritual direction that had been part of my training. All this reinforced my conviction that it would be impossible to relate my theology to the conservative conformism of most church congregations, ready to protest (so I thought) at any questioning of their faith. In a university setting I could use my own searching to raise and argue through questions of belief in my sermons and in discussion groups, and I found a ready response. The only students I seemed to offend were those in the Christian Union, which year by year sent a delegation to find out whether I believed in Jesus Christ as my Lord and Saviour. My answers, replete with qualifications as to what on earth that phrase meant, always sent them away convinced I was no Christian. I could see I would cause similar offence if I returned to a parish ministry.

I was changing direction; indeed, I had changed direction several times since starting working at Sussex. I was excited by exploration of what I was already calling inner space, following the type of ideas that Donald Winnicott had already been raising, although I did not know of his writing then. I was thinking more about psychological issues than the theological questions that had fired me at Oxford or the sociological and political questions in my first two years at Sussex.

Hugh Clegg then drew my attention to an opportunity for some more formal training, an *Introduction to Group Analysis* in London. Tony Ryle and Hugh were already going to attend, their fees paid by the university. But how was I to afford it? We had as a family kept in touch with David Toms, the registrar I had met when I was working in Walthamstow. He had moved about the same time as me to a hospital in Surrey and on one of the occasions we met I mentioned the course to him. I had not realised it but he and his wife had set up a trust fund to help people to train. They would pay my fees.

It was now 1971, and in the autumn of that year Hugh and I travelled up weekly together by train to London to attend the year-long course. It may have only been an introductory course but for me it was ground breaking. For the first two terms there were lectures from prominent group analysts in the first session of each day, followed by small group therapy for the second session. My group analyst was Robin Skynner (see Skynner and Cleese, 1983). Hugh and I were in different groups, and so I was for the first time on my own in this still new world. I thought of myself as entering the hallowed halls of psychoanalysis. I was not going to let on that I was a priest, despite the fact that there were a number of other priests on the course, and the wife of one in my group. I did not want to be pigeonholed by other group members. I am sure that would not have happened, but I recount this to show just how self-conscious I was of my background, and how mistaken I was about the prejudices of others.

My experience of group therapy was very different from anything I had experienced in my group relations training as a curate. Robin Skynner was human: he spoke about how he himself felt in the here-and-now, not as my previous consultants had as an outsider, but as a full member of the group. I remember these occasions more than any interpretations he might have made, since they were not obscure, but gave expression to what we were already feeling. He would laugh when he was amused, and would if necessary take the lead. He was such a different model from the fantasy picture I had built up of a psychoanalyst, and which I still had, despite my exposure to the student health service doctors. Robin Skynner and Eric Rayner, whom I was soon to see for my own therapy, provided two outstanding models that have shaped my whole style as a therapist.

In our third term the course leaders initiated an experiment of large group dynamics. I think it was the first year it had been introduced. Instead of lectures, all eighty participants and all the consultants on the course were in a large group, where I, in common with most, was too overawed to speak. But some did, and above all the consultants did, as they explored together (from chairs interspersed amongst us all) what they were thinking about and what they were feeling in the large group. It was again a fascinating experience, watching these analysts experiencing as much confusion as the rest of us, but trying to understand what was going on.

I was coming to the end of my fourth year at Sussex. There was only money for one more year, since I gathered Caffyn's Garages (whose shares financed my post) had taken a downturn. Daniel Jenkins had retired and his replacement as senior chaplain was a Church of Scotland and Church of South India minister, Duncan Forrester, a little older than myself. His wish, over and above his teaching, was to get involved with students and this made for some difficulties, since that was the very reason I had been appointed. We were in some instances treading on each other's toes. I wanted to leave early, before I was made redundant, and I started looking for university posts, fancying myself teaching pastoral theology, although I was not at all qualified to do so. It was the only way I could see of continuing to work in a university, and to engage with the two disciplines that really interested me.

Then, picking up a copy of *New Society* on Victoria Station on our way back from the group analysis course, Hugh Clegg spotted an advert for a post of psychological counsellor in the student health service at the University of Leicester. He pressured me to consider it, even though I myself thought that I stood no chance of getting it. He pointed out there was no harm in applying. So I submitted one application to the University of St Andrews for the post of lecturer in pastoral theology, and one to Leicester for the post of psychological counsellor. I asked Tony Ryle to be one of my referees for the latter post, since he knew the Leicester doctors through their membership of the British Association of Student Health.

I heard no more from St Andrews but I was shortlisted for the Leicester post. The interviews were postponed at

the last minute because the director of the Leicester service died suddenly. It was late June when I travelled with
my family to Nottingham to stay with David Toms and his
family, since he had now moved to Nottingham as a consultant, and I could make Leicester and back in a day.

It was an all-day affair, with mini-interviews in the
morning with the doctors, the retiring psychological counsellor and a consultant psychiatrist and psychoanalyst. In
the afternoon there was a high-level panel interview, with
the Vice-Chancellor, his deputy, the Dean of Medicine,
a Professor of Psychology and two of the health service
doctors. I met my fellow interviewees in the waiting area,
amongst them a social worker, a youth worker, and an
experienced psychotherapist already working part-time for
the service. I held out little hope that I stood a chance, and
perhaps that was why I was so bold in the interview. One
of the professors asked me how I would feel if one of my
patients were very anti-religious. I had the cheek to make
a type of transference interpretation: 'Would that be how
you are yourself?' I asked. He nodded. I cannot remember
the rest of my answer, but I knew one thing – I had one ally.
And when he left the post-interview discussion of the candidates early, he looked across in my direction and grinned.

To my utter surprise, I was called in and offered the
post. I went back to the health service building with the
two doctors, who made it clear that I had been their choice,
as I had apparently been the choice of the retiring counsellor and their consultant. I thought it would have been the
psychotherapist they wished to appoint, although when
we met a year or two later (his part-time post was not in
any case going to be continued) he thanked me for getting
the job, since he was not sure he had really wanted it, preferring his private practice.

I was, however, still a novice. I knew nothing then of the
wider field of counselling and psychotherapy that I have
referred to in these first two chapters. If I have conveyed
something of the influences upon me, and have mentioned

those who supported my development, I hope I have also made it obvious what a different world it was then. I was taking up a long-established post, where the retiring counsellor was a very experienced child psychotherapist (of whom more in the next chapter). I had received virtually no formal training. I certainly did not have (and never have had since) any formal qualifications. I had undertaken a one-year course of an introductory nature in group analysis; I had been supervised by a newly qualified psychotherapist; I had had experience of case discussions and theoretical seminars, and a small amount of knowledge through reading about psychoanalysis, which I had only just begun to make my own. And I had seen perhaps a dozen clients in all.

How had I got there? I had no doubt conveyed my enthusiasm to learn, and my love of the limited work I had experience of. I have seen in others whom I have trained since that time how this is more important than any formal qualification. Above all – so I was told by the acting director of the service, Jimmy Crighton, after the day's interviews – they thought I had potential. The university would pay for more training, and I would be supervised twice weekly by their consultant psychoanalyst, Isobel Hunter-Brown.

Many years later I came across an article where the author reflected on the development of psychoanalysis as a profession. In the 1950s, psychoanalysis in the United States was well established and perhaps at the height of its hegemonic hold on training. The psychoanalyst, Siegfried Bernfeld, who was thirty years on from his own brief training with Freud, addressed his own San Francisco psychoanalytic society. He questioned the way selection and personal analysis was then being conducted, and he concluded his lecture with the following thoughts:

> *It strikes me that the most natural way of selection would be the following: If I met someone who impressed me as interesting, talented, passionately*

interested in psychoanalysis, I would try to keep an eye on him. I would see him in seminars or at a party given by one of my colleagues, and I would have an opportunity to hear how he is doing with his psychiatric, psychotherapeutic, or medical cases. When my interest in him has continued for a reasonable length of time I would invite him to come as guest to the scientific meetings of the Psychoanalytic Society, and to the various seminars, lectures, and so on which the society or the institute is conducting. I would introduce him to my friends in the society and to some of the more experienced members, and I would draw their attention to this potential discovery. Some of them might have heard about him and observed him at his work, whatever that may be. Depending on the nature of his work we would invite him to give a lecture, participate in discussions, or give a paper; or, if he happens to be a psychotherapist, we would offer to control [supervise] some of his cases. Since he is interested in psychoanalysis he probably will be eager to be psychoanalyzed himself; and depending upon my time and the estimate of my countertransference I would take him for analysis myself or suggest that he get himself a place on someone else's schedule. After a certain time, let us say after one or two years, he will have established some social and professional contacts in addition to his meeting the group and to working with control analysts [supervisors]. A considerable part of the membership of the group will know by this time pretty well whether they like him, and whether they think he is or will be a good psychoanalyst or not. Accordingly, one day the group will vote him in or out.

(1962: 474–5)

What is remarkable is that this closely mirrors the way I came to be accepted as a psychodynamic counsellor and therapist some twenty years after he spoke. I had got to know a group of doctors who were working as psychotherapists, and I had begun working under supervision. I was not in any way formally trained, although I had read a lot of Freud. I had joined their seminars and case discussions. I was given a reference from a highly respected doctor who knew something of my work. I had not up to that point had any personal therapy. And I was voted in.

My experience was unusual but not unique at that time. None of that, I suspect, would ever happen now. When Bernfeld spoke, psychoanalysis, like most organisations, had developed a hardened system of rules, consisting of obstacles that had to be negotiated before anyone could practise as an analyst. Yet it was not like that at the beginning of psychoanalysis, nor was it like that when I was appointed to the post at Leicester. As later chapters will show, I deeply regret that counselling, like psychoanalysis, has gone so far along the same route.

3

A strange new world

On the day I was offered the post at Leicester and drove back to Nottingham to share my news with my family and the friends we were staying with, I was delighted as well as relieved, since I could now see a future ahead of me. But when we got back to Brighton, and I began to let people there know of my move, I became anxious and experienced feelings I had never had before. I had to put on an act of being pleased about the new job as people congratulated me. The Bishop of Horsham, Simon Phipps and the Archdeacon of Lewes, both of whom I got on very well with, were amongst them. It was not as if they disapproved of my move. But it was going to be a massive change of direction. The anxiety passed after three or so weeks, and I looked forward to starting in a new post and a new home in Leicester in October. I was fortunate that a grandparent had the year before left me a legacy that enabled me to put a deposit on a house, and the move went well.

However, in my second week in post the anxiety I had previously experienced returned and was far worse than before. I was on the verge of a breakdown: that I did not go under completely was because I was determined to continue working – and, strangely, I felt much better when

I was engaged with my student clients. It was not that I could not function as a therapist – which was of course a possibility given my lack of formal training. It was when I was face to face with a client that I felt most myself. That was the only part of my working day that was familiar to me; perhaps because my focus was on the client, and not on what was going on within me.

But I had very few clients: the first week I saw just four students whom my predecessor, Mary Swainson, had transferred to me. Only two of them returned the following week. The rest of the week I was virtually on my own, in a rather poorly lit room, with noisy traffic passing under the window. I had plenty to read, but I was becoming bored during the many hours I spent alone. My new colleagues, the doctors, were rushed off their feet, and although I saw them at lunchtime, and I visited my new supervisor Isobel Hunter-Brown twice a week, and attended a case seminar with the doctors at the end of the week, the contrast with my previous life was immense. Clients had to be referred to me by the doctors, as there was no open access, since this was the way my predecessor had worked, experienced though she was. This may have been as much for my protection as the clients, but it meant I began at a snail's pace. And whereas at Sussex I had had plenty of opportunities to do other things, such as mix with students, take services, and attend seminars and demonstrations, here I was cut off like a Cistercian monk. I was the only counsellor – quite a contrast to today's counselling services where there is usually a supportive team. That was not in itself unusual at the time, since most counsellors worked in relative isolation. While the doctors were supportive, they were not generally available, and, in any case, their surgeries were on the ground floor, while I was alone upstairs. I did some months later change my room for a long narrow one at the back of the building that at least had the virtue of being both light and quiet.

I also started that first week on the course upon which I had been enrolled, travelling down to London to the

Tavistock Clinic. Two of the doctors had attended or were attending a course in psychotherapy designed specifically for GPs, and Jimmy Crighton, now the director of the student health service, wanted me to attend the parallel course for clinical psychologists. I was accepted on the course, but the others were all clinical psychologists and I immediately felt different, having had nothing like the training of my fellow students. I could not face going the second week, and I poured out how distressed I felt to my boss. I think he was right when he said that I was having an identity crisis, an interpretation he was very used to making when working with so many young people (and indeed it was rather a popular one at the time, but no less the useful to me at that point for all that). I certainly did not know who I was. And although I was working quite well in face-to-face counselling, I did lack the confidence that had always been part of me before.

Furthermore, I felt isolated from the Church, however much I had kicked against it. Disillusioned as I was with the Church and my previous theological position, I was taking a major step away from 'mother' church into a purely secular role. This was made worse by the attitude of the then Bishop of Leicester, Ronald Williams. I had written to him and asked for permission to officiate. This meant that I would have had a licence from him to function as a priest in his diocese, although I told him that I intended to keep a low profile. It would mean that I would be loosely attached to the diocese while working in a secular role. I told him I would be a kind of worker-priest, similar to those in France who had taken off their dog-collars and gone to work in factories alongside other employees. Looking back I can see that had I had this attachment it would have made quite a difference to me, helping the transition I was making; and it could eventually have turned out to be some advantage to the Church, since I might have been able to make a particular contribution behind the scenes, as I was to do later.

The bishop asked to see me, and having heard me out told me I could not have my cake and eat it, and refused to license me. In what seemed like an empty gesture to me, he insisted I kneel and he bless me. This was so different from the response to my move that I had had from Simon Phipps, the Bishop of Horsham. But there was a third element to my sense of isolation: while I had intended to attend my local church as an ordinary member of the congregation, I found that experience, after the services I had helped lead in the university chapel, was dull and irritating, with sermons that were for the most part rather shallow.

My wife Valerie was inevitably thrown by my distress, since she had thought this move was one that I had wanted. She had also given up the role of a clergy wife with its attendant activities, even if like many others in a similar position she had been an 'unpaid curate'. I was the breadwinner, with a new mortgage, having never owned a property before; and I had three children who did not need a distressed father. Fortunately, home and family were to some extent a distraction, although for a long while the inner turmoil never completely went away. I woke in an anxious state each morning, and felt queasy until I actually got to work. Yet looking back, what I was going through made a huge difference to me both personally and professionally.

Personally I was experiencing what I had never knowingly experienced before, a sense of my own fragility, the soft underbelly of the always-confident person I had thought myself to be up to that point. Professionally, my own experience helped me to become much more sensitive to and appreciative of the distress of those I was to work with. They may have presented in many different ways, but that sense of losing hold of oneself is an inevitable part of emotional and psychological turmoil. The depth of my experience, even when it was replaced by what Freud called 'common unhappiness', has stayed with me enough to influence the way I work, since empathy is central to being a therapist, and empathy is deeply enhanced by personal identification.

My supervisor Isobel Hunter-Brown had recommended the first week I saw her that I enter personal therapy, but I could not afford to do so, what with a new mortgage and family commitments. When I saw her in the second week, no longer feeling fine, I agreed that I would have to see someone, and she arranged for me to see a fellow analyst, Eric Rayner, when I was down in London on my Tavistock course. He offered me a reduced fee, which I could just afford, and he agreed to longer breaks covering those times when I was not attending the course, since my university was also paying my fares to London on days the course met. That flexibility was something that I deeply appreciated at the time, and it has been a feature of my own work since when flexibility is really needed by a client. What was even more important was that I now felt safe, knowing, as so many of our clients do, that however hard a particular day might be, I would see him each week.

Looking back, it was the best way to enter therapy, better than having therapy because it was a good thing to do, as had been suggested in my supervision with Isobel. My later experience of working with one or two of the trainees who were in therapy with me as part of their course requirements has felt to me on occasion as if we are going through the motions, scratching around on the surface, trying to find something significant to work on. Years later, when a London-trained psychotherapist moved to Leicester, and argued that twice a week therapy was essential to help break down defences, I replied that in my experience most people entering therapy of their own accord had already had their defences broken down. However, some trainees can remain very defended. I have since written about this issue (2011).

My defences were certainly shattered. It took me two years to feel confident that I was getting on my feet again. I had entered a strange outer world but also a strange new inner world, which of course was one I would never leave, however much I became used to it. I had another blip at the start of my fourth year at Leicester, because of personal circumstances that were only obliquely related to the job, which brought more distress and showed me another side of myself. But I was by then firmly in my role, and my experience as a counsellor and psychotherapist gradually became richer.

What also helped the transition from priest to therapist from the start was membership of two associations, the Association of Student Counsellors (ASC) and the Association for Pastoral Care and Counselling (APCC), both of which I joined as soon as I had made the move to Leicester. Both were relatively new organisations, since both student counselling and pastoral counselling in Britain were themselves relatively new interests. I say more about my membership of the APCC in the later chapters.

The ASC had only been inaugurated in 1970. It had developed from an initiative in 1966 by students on full-time counselling courses at Keele and Reading when they formed the National Association of Educational Counsellors. As I have indicated previously, there were still only a handful of counsellors in universities in 1972, although the post that I now occupied was the oldest. My predecessor, Mary Swainson, had been appointed a lecturer in geography at the then University College of Leicester in 1948, but in fact her role was to be a therapist to student teachers. She was a member of the British Association of Psychotherapists. A professor of education, Professor Tibble, had realised that if student teachers could achieve better mental health, this would rub off on those they taught. His foresight extended also to inviting the Tavistock Institute of Human Relations to Leicester for its group relations conferences, conferences that took place throughout my time there.

Mary's role as a counsellor and therapist was disguised initially because of the suspicion about therapy that existed elsewhere in the university in 1948. In 1972, I too found some staff, whom we might call the 'stiff-upper-lip' brigade, who asked about my position in the university and then said that they had 'never needed such a thing in my day'. Even when Mary came out of the shadows, joining the student health service team when it started in 1967, she was called 'psychological counsellor' because the prefix 'psychological' tempered what would otherwise be regarded as a very American term (Swainson, 1977). She had worked from her home near the halls of residence, so my office being situated as it was on campus (actually slightly off campus) was a move towards making counselling more visible. I too started as the 'psychological counsellor', although I soon dropped the adjective 'psychological' in my self-description, and later added 'psychotherapist'.

Leicester therefore had the first counselling service of any British university, although Keele likes to claim it was the first. Keele's was perhaps the first to be clearly advertised as such, when Audrey Newsome, a careers officer at Keele, trained as a counsellor in America and then added counselling to her careers and appointments service in 1964. Perhaps the honours can be shared: Leicester the first appointment, Keele the first service.

Audrey Newsome soon had other staff working with her, although I cannot recall whether Brian Thorne, one of her team, was still at Keele or had moved to head up a new service at the University of East Anglia when I first met him. I had attended a conference for university chaplains when I was at Sussex, where he led a session on Carl Rogers, showing the film of Rogers working with Gloria. As those who have seen the film might recall, Rogers was warm and generous in his responses to her. The majority of us at Brian's session had not come across anything like this before, and my own impression was that Rogers was almost bending over backwards to praise and complement her. When the filmed interview itself came to an end and Rogers appeared to camera to comment on his work, instead of being smartly dressed as in the interview, he was now in shirtsleeves with an open collar. I'm afraid the salacious minds of the clergy interpreted this change as if Rogers had just emerged from a very different type of session with Gloria and laughter rippled through the room. Brian appeared deeply puzzled by their reaction. It was indeed inappropriate, but I have often wondered whether the reaction to that film prejudiced me initially against Rogers.

When I joined ASC, and later, I was to value Brian Thorne's huge contribution to the development of counselling, and at various times his personal support. At one time the Leicester Students Union wanted to appoint their own independent counsellor outside the student health service, whom students could approach without needing a medical referral. Brian wrote a strong letter in support of my position; and the doctors realised at the same time that I could no longer be confined to only seeing students referred to me by them. There was thereafter a policy of open access. Eventually, when I moved to the Department of Adult Education and Moira Walker became head of counselling, the counselling service had its own new wing built on to the medical building with its own entrance, independent of and yet working cooperatively with the health centre.

Brian Thorne was a key figure in ASC, and in the early 1990s when he and I were no longer active in the association we were invited to run a day together at the ASC's annual conference to promote dialogue between the person-centred and psychodynamic members. Workshops were led on a number of topics by facilitators from both camps, and the two of us spent much of the day together preparing for the final session, where we were to discuss our differences. In fact, we were both long enough in the tooth to be relaxed about where we parted company, and we were more interested in the commonalities, while respecting and valuing some of the points where we seemed to diverge.

Nevertheless, the tension between the two principal modalities in counselling was evident when I attended my first ASC conference at the end of the first year at Leicester.

There was a division between those counsellors like myself who were psychoanalytic in orientation and those who were person-centred. The former tended to be linked to university medical services, and were sometimes also members of the British Student Health Association. Although membership of ASC was still small in 1973, I initially felt quite a stranger in a group of people who seemed to know each other rather well, especially when I found myself under fire from some of the person-centred members because I used the term 'patient' instead of 'client'. (Neither term seems to me satisfactory, although I have given in to the prevailing fashion and tend to use the term 'client' now.) Other aspects of my orientation were also questioned.

This tension between modalities has always existed and will no doubt continue to exist. Many years later, Brian Thorne engaged me to take an afternoon's session on psychodynamic counselling for a residential course he was running. I was given a hard time and experienced considerable aggression in the response I had from the participants. When I discussed this with Brian afterwards, I felt reassured when he put their aggressive response all down to transference! Those learning a counselling modality for the first time – and perhaps for a few years afterwards – tend to be evangelistic and suspicious of anything other than the pure gospel of Rogers, Freud or their particular saint. I was no exception in those early years with a strong conviction that the psychoanalytic approach was superior to any other. In time I was to prefer the term 'psychodynamic' as being less precious and less divisive.

My training at the Tavistock Clinic was psychoanalytic, but it was broad, since psychoanalysis is itself what might be called a broad church. There have been three particular divisions in British psychoanalysis, the Freudians, the Kleinians and the Middle or Independent Groups, with all manner of different emphases even within those groupings. My therapist Eric Rayner was of the independent group, which was just right for me. He was also my first lecturer on the Tavistock course, followed by a Reichian, John Steiner, and then sessions with John Bowlby, John Padel, Ellen Noonan (who was to go on to inaugurate the Birkbeck College courses) and others who were known to me by their writing. To listen to them and appreciate them in person was important – and de-mystifying. But when I started therapy with Eric Rayner, he was still lecturing to the course and this presented a particularly interesting boundary issue. Although he was a fine therapist and an excellent author, he was a dreadful teacher – communicating what was essentially good material in a hesitant and convoluted manner. If I was going to be open with him in therapy, I could not suppress my criticism of his teaching style. Distressed though I was, I knew that I would not get rid of that nagging criticism of him unless I got it out of the way and told him. When I did so, he was unshaken, relaxed and probably rather pleased that I had been able to voice some negative feelings. It did not detract at all from everything I learned from him about a style of relating that was open, warm and receptive.

The two-year Tavistock course carried no paper qualifications with it – something that was to cause difficulty for me later when BACP registration became so dependent on paper evidence. When the course ended I continued to have twice-weekly supervision with Isobel Hunter-Brown, eventually dropping down to once weekly until she retired in the early 1980s. The learning that can come from good supervision stayed with me, so that when Moira Walker and I started our psychotherapy course at Leicester, we required students to be in weekly supervision outside the course, as well as take part in supervision triads weekly on the course. We believed this to be of greater value than the obligatory twice-weekly personal therapy that many other psychoanalytic and psychodynamic psychotherapy trainings required.

When Isobel retired, I continued to attend the weekly supervision group, which had developed out of the weekly meeting of the doctors in the service. The Friday seminar gradually shifted in its membership so that only the doctors interested in psychotherapy attended when they could, while the majority of members of the group were counsellors and chaplains at both the universities in Leicester and any students on placement with us. These were really important meetings in my early years, although I came in time to find the routine of one person presenting each week rather sterile. When in the 1990s Moira Walker and I taught supervision courses, I developed a number of ways of using group supervision that proved to be much more testing and valuable than what I came to call 'French cricket' – that is (for those who know the game and might see the parallel), one person presenting while the other members of the group toss ideas at the presenter for the him or her to address, rather like batting away a ball that can come from any direction. That felt too much like an opportunity for group members to demonstrate their insights, while the poor presenter tried to field their questions and absorb all their comments and clever interpretations. I explain these other methods of group supervision in the book on supervision that Moira Walker and I wrote together (2004: 117–24).

When I eventually moved from my counselling post to Adult Education and then saw up to four clients a week as a volunteer at the Leicester Counselling Centre, I naturally ceased to attend the group. Like many experienced therapists, I really did not see the need for compulsory supervision. It had been usual in psychoanalytic training to lessen the requirement for supervision once a person had been accepted as a member of the Institute. If I had not learned through my internal supervisor how to monitor my work after fourteen years and some thousand sessions a year, I really could not be much of a therapist. Of course, if I came up against an issue I could talk it over with a colleague, as I did with Moira Walker and she likewise could talk to me, without having to identify the name of the client. Such informal conversations would often throw light on the issue in the same way supervision should do. Furthermore, I had to supervise students on placement without any specific training for supervising, since there was none in those days. Supervision was not just a place of learning for my supervisees, but also for myself. In that context, supervisor and supervisee can say things as they are, whereas in therapy, interventions have to be thought about, even if it is only in a split second, and made understandable to the client. Carrying over that frankness of the supervision experience into thinking before you speak in therapy makes a great difference to the work.

Within a few years of being in post, my professional life was expanding. No longer was I isolated in the counselling room all week, since I began to sit on committees, to write and to take placement students. I had the model of my own supervision to draw upon, although I think I was less wedded to a pure psychoanalytic doctrine than Isobel Hunter-Brown appeared to be. I may be unfair to her, since she could be described as very thorough. But I came to question some of her interpretations, and to be wary of always taking her advice. One piece of advice I did take from her I have always regretted, and I think was one of the biggest mistakes in my career. A client, who was still in therapy, had given me a book as a Christmas present. (The question of gifts is a really interesting one, which I have since addressed in one of my lectures.) Isobel advised me to return the book, while seeking to understand the significance of the gift for the client. I may have taken my supervisor's prompting too literally, when she was in fact observing one possible way of dealing with the gift, but I returned the book at the next session. There was no opportunity to discuss its significance since the client immediately stormed out of the room. Although she came back towards the end of the session, the damage had been done. She literally threw the torn-up book at me. We only just survived the ruction my action had caused, and I think it intensified the relationship between us unnecessarily, taking it much longer to resolve. I included that example when Windy Dryden invited me to contribute to the book on *Hard-Earned Lessons from Counselling in Action* (1992: 58–68), in relation to the incident where I said that while I did not blame my supervisor, who was technically correct, I learned the need to believe my own assessment of the situation.

Unlike most counselling services in other universities, my own did not expand its staffing during my time working in the student health service. The Leicester Polytechnic, soon to become the De Montfort University, had appointed Jean Clark a year before I started, and eventually had three counsellors. Loughborough appointed Bernard Ratigan the year after I went to Leicester and another, Alan Lilley, soon after that. Bernard was a therapist for whom I had the utmost respect. I was also somewhat in awe of him, and after I had retired and returned to give a lecture in Leicester where he was present, I said to him that I had always seen him as a much deeper thinker than myself. He responded that for him it had been the other way round, that he had seen me as superior to him! What strange beings we are, and what projections we are prone to!

The counsellors at universities in the East Midlands area began to meet regularly for what would now be called away-days. These sometimes took the form of training, sometimes of discussions of policy. As other universities in the area made counselling appointments and new counsellors joined us, it began to feel as though we were sometimes going over old ground afresh, but that was perhaps inevitable with such a rapid expansion of services.

That my own service did not expand its permanent staffing during my time in it is partly my own fault, because I did not push hard enough for more help. My supervisor was also seeing students, normally those with more severe mental health problems, and since she was employed as a consultant to the student health service, the university was not keen to expand any further. But my caseload began to grow extensively, so that when Windy Dryden, then teaching a full-time counselling course at Aston University, got in touch with me and asked if I would take a placement student, I readily consented. There was one difficulty, however – the student was expected to tape sessions, something I was at that time totally against, since I saw the presence of a tape recorder as interfering with the therapeutic relationship. But I was adamant, so the student had to undertake a second placement elsewhere to comply with the regulation. Windy and I made our respective positions clear in BAC's journal *Counselling* (Jacobs, 1981a: 10–13; Dryden, 1981: 14–17).

I was later to partly change my mind (1993b: 4–8) and by the mid-1990s I was requiring four taped sessions as part of the assessment for our *Certificate in Psychodynamic Supervision*. There is, I have come to recognise, so much to be learned from such tapes, allowing a tutor (or a supervisor) to provide much better feedback. It must of course be done with the client's consent, and with ongoing awareness of the presence and influence of the recorder. I was to use such taping when I worked on my book *In Search of Supervision* (1996a) where my client in that book found the tapes very useful. If we are going to record, then it is only fair that the client should be offered a copy of each recording, as was Windy's practice. I had one client who herself wanted to tape the sessions, as an understandable precaution against my abusing her, arising from her previous experience. I think it was useful for her too to play the tapes back; and on one occasion, when we disputed what she thought I had said earlier in the session, I did suggest she would find I was right in my recall when she played back the tape. I was!

In preparation for the first student placement from Aston, Windy's colleague Richard Nelson-Jones visited the service and he attended our weekly case seminar, checking out our credentials. His orientation at the time was person-centred, although later he moved more towards cognitive-behavioural therapy. My supervisor Isobel Hunter-Brown clearly was suspicious about some of his contributions to the discussion, person-centred counselling being quite foreign to her. In a delightful Freudian slip, she addressed him every time as 'Dr Elsan-Jones' – Elsan, as campers may know, being a type of portable toilet.

In time I had students from other courses on placement, many coming from a person-centred background. By the time I was ready to move on to the Department of Adult Education in the university, I had two people working with me on placement: a counsellor who had moved to the area and wanted to continue her experience while she looked for a post; and Dominic Davies, a young youth work student, who proved to be a real boon to the service. Both of them applied for my job when it was advertised, although neither got it (Moira Walker was appointed). Dominic did very well in his interview, but it was thought he needed more experience. In fact, he had more experience than I had when I was appointed to the post in 1972, which is in itself an indication of how far things had moved on in fourteen years. Moira Walker was not able to start straightaway, and it was reassuring to be able to offer Dominic a temporary post to head up the service until she arrived. He has since gone on to make a major contribution to counselling and therapy in the LGBT field, producing three books on working with LGBT clients for me during my period of editorial consultancy at Open University Press (Davies and Neal, 1996, 2000; Neal and Davies, 2000).

When the time came for me to leave the counselling service, I had myself come a long way. I had been changing all the time. From those isolated days in a strange new world, working with a handful of clients, I had at times had a caseload of upwards of thirty clients each week, some for one or two sessions, some for three years or more, and many more in between. I find it strange that Employee Assistance Programmes and NHS counselling have a strict limit of five or six sessions, since my experience over those fourteen years working full time as a counsellor was that if clients are given the option of the number of sessions they wish or feel the need for, the average number of sessions year on year was only six. The flexibility I had then of being able to offer the client what the client wanted, or what assessment suggested might be appropriate, allowed for working short, middle and long term; and there was seldom a waiting list. Of course since that time the demand for counselling has mushroomed, and university numbers have vastly expanded, yet it seems strange to me that some university counselling services can now only offer one or two sessions.

It was not only myself who had come a long way. At the same time the whole counselling scene was growing, and would continue to grow. It was no longer thought that counselling was a soft option, since it was now being described routinely as available following traumatic incidents. I found myself once again with a variety of opportunities, albeit different ones from those that I had desperately missed when I left Sussex and started at Leicester. I had initiated counselling training in the university's adult education programme, a major part of the next fifteen years at Leicester. I return to that aspect of my career in Chapter 5. I had had an article and a book published, the start of my work as a writer, which Chapter 6 discusses. And, as the next chapter describes, I had already been making a contribution to the development of the British Association for Counselling.

4

Early years in the British Association for Counselling

Towards the end of the 1990s, I approached Alan Jamieson, then acting chief executive of the British Association for Counselling (BAC as it was then), to see whether the management committee would permit me to work from its archives on a history of the organisation. Living in Leicester made it convenient for me to travel to Rugby to work on the documentation stored in BAC's offices. I presume permission was granted, because I visited Alan in order to start my research. We descended into the basement of 1 Regency Place, Rugby and found what can only be described as a chaotic jumble of papers, which no one had thought to order. By chance we discovered a minute book from the Standing Conference for the Advancement of Counselling (SCAC) for 1977. Alan deposited me in a spare office with the minutes, which I proceeded to read.

I turned first to some SCAC minutes that were, I believe, from March 1976, where there was a record of a discussion about requests from individual counsellors to be admitted to membership of the Standing Conference. Founded in 1970,

SCAC only admitted organisations into membership. The minutes record the view that if individuals were allowed into membership, they could then use membership as if it was a qualification for counselling. This was undesirable since there was no way of assessing them. The decision was made not to change the membership requirement.

I read the next set of minutes, dated three months later. Here the treasurer was reported as saying that SCAC could not survive financially. After some discussion it was decided that the only way of becoming economically viable was to admit individual members! My memory of these minutes is bolstered by Nicholas Tyndall, vice-chair of SCAC at the time, who wrote that the reason for the formation of the British Association for Counselling was financial, since the Home Office grant to SCAC was insufficient to meet its needs (1993: 9).

The state of the archives was such that it put me off taking my project any further. It would have been far too time-consuming trying to sort through the disordered piles of paper, a situation which I hope BACP may have rectified since with the appointment of a proper archivist. It is essential for an organisation to know its history if it is not to go on re-inventing the wheel. The evidence of a video on YouTube about BACP (https://www.youtube.com/watch?v=PzLz0JsOz0Y) is that it is thought that BAC started over a butcher's shop in Rugby. This was in fact the third set of offices that BAC occupied, when it had already been in existence for six or seven years. The history that I proposed has not yet been written, although in this chapter I share my own recall of the years I was involved at the centre of BAC.

What struck me at the time of reading the SCAC minutes was how readily caution about admitting individual members to a national organisation was thrown to the winds when money became the main issue. Pragmatism gives way too easily to principles, although sometimes, to be fair, principles prevent pragmatism. BACP has since attempted to ensure that membership means something, although I shall have occasion in this chapter and my final chapter to question whether it has also excluded those who in the early days were interested in how they might adapt counselling skills and insights for use in other caring professions. If we examine the origins of BAC (this was 23 years before becoming BACP), it is clear that the origins of counselling in Britain were firmly in the voluntary sector, a long way from the way in which BACP has become an organisation for professionals. The voluntary element has always been just as important to me and in all I have tried to promote, as well as being 'professional' in the sense of working to as high a standard as possible. Many of the pioneers of counselling in Britain, including myself, came either from the voluntary sector or from a profession other than counselling.

Although there is as yet no official history of counselling, valuable historical information can be found in the series *Counselling in Context*, edited in the 1990s by Moira Walker and myself. These books were largely written by those who had experienced at first hand the development of counselling in various settings in the United Kingdom (Tyndall, 1993; Syme, 1994; Brearley, 1995; Lyall, 1995; Mabey and Sorensen, 1995; Bell, 1996). There is also a useful set of papers in the *British Journal of Guidance and Counselling* (Volume 28(4)) by myself (2000b), Windy Dryden, Dave Mearns and Brian Thorne (2000), and A.G. Watts and Jennifer Kidd (2000).

Counselling as we know it (as distinct from counsel in the broader sense) has been a feature of British culture since the founding of the National Marriage Guidance Council (NMGC) in 1938, although its initial purpose was to provide lectures on marriage and the family. Yet by 1946, NMGC (later to become Relate) was selecting volunteer counsellors through a stringent process that was based on War Office selection of officers during the Second World War. Those accepted underwent a year's compulsory training programme. These counsellors were more like assessors referring people on to appropriate professional help, but gradually they began to become the main helpers themselves. Not long afterwards, in 1953, the Reverend Chad Varah founded the Samaritans, albeit offering befriending rather than counselling as such.

Another major development was in the churches. In 1959, the Scottish Pastoral Association was founded, developing its own journal, *Contact*, launched in 1960. Frank Lake founded the Clinical Theology Association in 1962. A Methodist minister, Bill Kyle, started the Highgate Counselling Centre (London) in 1960 and went on to found the Westminster Pastoral Foundation in 1965, which in turn expanded for many years into a series of affiliated branches throughout the country. The Roman Catholics had their own London counselling centre, the Dympna Centre, founded by Father Louis Marteau in 1971, which was an ecumenical enterprise that embraced different religious traditions. The Salvation Army had also by this time started its own counselling service and training of its officers. There were a number of Church of England dioceses, such as Southwark and Rochester, which had appointed directors of pastoral care and counselling (Lyall, 1995: 1–29).

I have already referred in the previous chapter to the Association of Student Counsellors (ASC), one of the first organisations I joined when I moved to Leicester. In 1970, it had about forty members, although ten years later this number had grown to about 500 members, as most universities and many colleges of further education recognised the value of counselling to stem the costs of student wastage. Here again it was an economic argument that helped the development of such services. There were also an increasing number of trained counsellors in secondary schools. By 1977, there were 351 specialist counsellors working in schools in England and Wales, although from this point on there was a decline in numbers as more teachers were trained in pastoral care as part of their role (Mabey and Sorensen, 1995: 10).

Paul Halmos, in *The Faith of the Counsellors*, first published in 1965, records about 5650 people in caring roles – including psychiatrists, psychoanalysts, psychologists and social workers, although interestingly, despite the title of his book, there was as yet no specific category of 'counsellor' in his initial computation. In the second edition of his book in 1978, Halmos assesses that there were 21,350 people in the caring professions, of whom 800 were counsellors. This certainly is an underestimate of the number of counsellors, but the differences between the two editions indicate a huge increase in interest in the late 1960s and 1970s both in counselling itself and in some of the basic principles that inform counselling. As defined by Halmos, these principles were (and it might well be argued still are): the combination of a warm spontaneous relationship and carefully thought-out technique; the need for both personal involvement as well as objectivity; and the paradox of non-directiveness on the one hand and an educative element on the other (Brearley, 1995: 2; see also Halmos, 1965).

It was in the light of these developments in different areas that the Standing Conference for the Advancement of Counselling (SCAC) was set up in 1970, drawing in voluntary and professional bodies as organisational members. I am not sure I knew much if any of its existence, since my own interests were met by ASC on the one hand, and the Association of Pastoral Care and Counselling (APCC) on the other. APCC pulled together the type of initiatives in the churches described above. Tyndall describes the original 'divisions' in the SCAC as: ASC, APCC and Counselling in Education, with other divisions formed later for counselling in medical settings, workplace counselling, youth counselling and a division that drew together voluntary organisations not in other groupings, the Personal, Sexual, Marriage and Family Division. However, the youth counselling division, the National Association for Young

People's Counselling and Advisory Services (NAYPCAS), broke away in 1975 (Tyndall, 1993: 8–9).

I have already described the circumstances that led to the transformation of SCAC into the British Association for Counselling in 1977. As a member of both ASC and APCC, I attended the debate within each association as to whether or not to become a division of BAC. Each organisation questioned whether it might lose a certain amount of independence by such a move. In my opinion at the time, it would also mean joining a third organisation and paying yet another membership fee to BAC as well as to ASC and APCC – yes, economics dictated my views as well! I had an additional concern about APCC, which anticipated and still represents my main concern about the way counselling has developed as a profession, that many of APCC's members were parish clergy, whose interest was primarily in pastoral care and not necessarily in pastoral counselling. APCC could lose such members (and indeed to some extent did) becoming an association linked loosely to the church where the main interest was counselling or psychotherapy. I voted at the extraordinary general meetings held by ASC and APCC against joining BAC.

ASC's meeting was held in October 1976. Elsa Bell describes how Brian Thorne, the chair, remembered it as 'a painful and tense occasion' (1996: 24). The arguments aired were divided between those who felt that joining BAC would help raise standards of counselling everywhere, and those who felt that joining an organisation that accepted everyone would undermine the development of high standards of practice and training in ASC itself. In the event, I decided that I would resign my membership of ASC and throw in my lot with APCC, even if it would inevitably involve becoming a member of BAC as well.

Looking back in the year 2000, Dryden, Mearns and Thorne are sanguine about BAC, appearing to support in their own way my concerns about the development of counselling. They comment that there is 'a danger that what was once a pioneering and creative activity pursued by the talented few will become an institutionalised, rule-bound and essentially stultifying pursuit which loses the vitality and imaginative élan on which it depends for its effectiveness and healing power' (2000: 471). In the same context, they reflect on the way 'the vigorous "professionalisation" of counselling that has gathered irresistible momentum in recent years does not sit altogether comfortably in the historical evolution of an activity which . . . has many of its roots in the voluntary sector' (2000: 471).

This was not just my own worry at the time. It must have been in the minds of the editors of BAC's first journal *Counselling* in April 1981. The theme of the issue is 'Aspects of professionalism', and the short editorial states that 'professionalism is a word which can arouse some anxieties in BAC members. We are a comprehensive organisation and at one end of the spectrum we have those who see themselves as befrienders and pastoral carers. While at the other end there are highly trained psychiatrists and psychotherapists' (*Counselling*, 36: 1). I wonder whether BACP with its current requirement that all members other than students and those who have retired must be registered still includes befrienders, members of caring professions (who are not trained as counsellors) and pastoral carers in its membership?

Concern for the narrowing of counselling in the new organisation was reflected in the decision of NAYPCAS to vigorously oppose the formation of BAC. One of my clearest memories of the extraordinary general meeting of SCAC where the resolution to become BAC was debated, is that NAYPCAS's representatives were the most vocal in their opposition. They argued that advisory services should be included alongside counselling, but more importantly they too saw counselling as primarily carried out by people in the voluntary sector. I do not recall how I voted on that occasion, but if there was a vote, I probably bowed to the inevitable.

It might be considered hypocritical on my part to want to champion volunteers. After all, like most members of ASC I was receiving a salary and I was eager to be identified as a professional counsellor and therapist, more so then than I do now. But as Dryden et al. (2000: 469) observe, at that time, not only were many in APCC working in a voluntary capacity, but also those of us who were student counsellors did not charge fees, and our clients did not have to pay. This principle of access to free counselling (or in some voluntary organisations, low-cost counselling) meant that even then there was a concern that with the formation of this national association, professionalisation would encourage those who wanted to make a living out of counselling by charging fees, and that the values present up to that point in the counselling movement would take second place. Although until I retired I was salaried as a counsellor, my energies have been devoted from that secure base to the development and support of voluntary counselling centres and the training of volunteers in counselling, as well as in enhancing the work of other caring profession through introducing them to counselling skills. While there is much that BAC(P) has achieved in the professionalisation of counselling in the better sense of raising of the standards and profile of counselling, I remain concerned that the voluntary element has taken second place. Recently I took heart when BACP circulated a celebration of National Volunteers Week, saying that much had been achieved through the dedication and commitment of their volunteers – but it was *their* volunteers, those giving their time to BACP, without recognition of the hundreds of volunteer counsellors in Britain.

It was a good move to continue the divisions that had been part of SCAC in the structure of the BAC (still minus, apart from a division for counsellors in schools, young people's counselling). It is instructive to compare this structure with the later Standing Conference on Psychotherapy and the UK Council for Psychotherapy. BAC's divisions, for those who chose to join one, were related to counselling settings rather than to modalities. There may have been debates about the similarities and differences between modalities, as I described in connection with ASC in Chapter 3. But there has never been the same degree of competition between modalities that I have encountered elsewhere and which has I believe bogged down the development of an umbrella group that embraces psychoanalysis, psychotherapy and counselling, the latter two groupings representing many different orientations. Professionalisation in its worst sense leads to the defence of professional interests over and above defence of service to those in need.

Membership of BAC did not depend upon having to join a division, so it could attract into membership those whose interest was counselling but who did not have a particular allegiance to one modality or setting. On the other hand, one of the strengths of the UK Council for Psychotherapy (UKCP), where most of its members join through prior membership of training organisations and psychotherapy institutes, is that their continuing registration and review is through smaller units where largely they are known personally, whereas registration and review in BACP has become a bureaucratic computer-controlled exercise.

The growth of BAC(P) has been astonishing, although I still look back fondly to those early days when as many as ten per cent of its members would come together for annual general meetings and conferences. As BAC began to fledge its wings in 1977, it had 1400 individual members. The literature includes various estimates of the increasing numbers of members. Gabrielle Syme records 1858 members in 1979/80 (1994: 9), although in an address to the Institute of Psychiatry in 1980, BAC's chair, Audrey Newsome, speaks of 2400 individual members and 190 organisational members (1980: 103). There is more agreement on the situation ten years later, Syme citing 7218 individual members in 1990/91 (1994: 9) and Tyndall nearly 7500 individual members and 450 organisational members in 1992 (1993: 9). Tyndall estimates that the division that contained most of the voluntary counsellors had 900 members in 1992 (1993: 9–10).

I was really not interested in BAC for the first two years of its existence. My focus outside Leicester was on my membership of APCC, where, as I describe in Chapter 6, I was beginning in 1976 to take on various responsibilities to do with publications. Being part of APCC was one of the factors that helped me retain something of my old identity. It enabled me to sustain my relationship with like-minded people in the churches, including clergy whom I had known from theological college and from the group analysis course I attended. Some were in similar specialist ministries, such as chaplains in mental hospitals.

I had become a member of APCC at the prompting of a priest, Leslie Virgo, with whom I had worked in my vacations while an undergraduate at Oxford, and who it will be seen was rather a significant figure in my career development. As I record in these pages, he proposed me for various roles that I would not otherwise have put myself forward for. Leslie had taught me much as a student and he showed enormous generosity of spirit. When I informed him of my move to Leicester, he drew my attention to the association that up to that point I had not heard of. He had become the Adviser in Pastoral Care and Counselling in the diocese of Rochester, and he became APCC's representative on the first BAC management committee.

So, I knew little of BAC in 1977 and most of 1978. Nicholas Tyndall, Director of Marriage Guidance, was the new chair, retiring from that office at the AGM in 1978. Another pioneer of long standing, Audrey Newsome, became the new chair, with Mary Godden, a marriage guidance counsellor, as vice-chair. It was then that Leslie asked me to take over his role and represent APCC on the management committee. This was perhaps because a move to Rugby was in the air, making it more convenient for me in Leicester to attend meetings.

Meetings of the management committee were initially held in London, where BAC was located in an office basement in a London square. The BACP website only lists general secretaries and chief executives from 1982, but previously there were two general managers, the first of whom was London based. I cannot recall her name or that of her assistant, although I do remember being invited by them to take part in a visit to the Isis Centre in Oxford. The centre had opened within the NHS on the initiative of psychiatrists Dr Peter Agulnik and Dr Bertram Mandelbrote and received its first clients in 1971 (Agulnik et al., 1976). It is still in existence today and, according to one website, it still offers free counselling and psychotherapy on the NHS. The coordinator at that time of our visit in 1977 or 1978 was Susan Oldfield, who describes the work of the Isis Centre in more detail in her book *The Counselling Relationship* (1983).

The reason the visit stays in my memory is that in hearing about their work I wanted to develop a similar counselling centre in Leicester. It was perhaps this that impelled me into more interest in BAC, since I thought that the association might support such a project.

BAC relocated to two rooms within Marriage Guidance's offices in Rugby in 1978 and a new general manager, Doreen Schofield, was appointed. I imagine the initiative to move to Rugby was due to Nick Tyndall. Although he had retired as chair, I remember him taking an active interest in BAC, since he was often present at some point during my own frequent visits to the Rugby offices.

Doreen Schofield's first meeting with the management committee was when it met for the last time in London, and by chance we walked back to our respective trains together. I was impressed by her enthusiasm, and I think she realised that I had an agenda, my counselling centre idea, that could involve BAC. I am not generally a good committee member since I tend to get rather bored by talk and more talk about what can often seem mundane business. Since she was new in the post and wanted to put BAC on the map, my idea appealed to her.

We spoke more on the phone the next day and I visited the new Rugby offices. It was the start of what was largely a productive working relationship, as well as a good friendship, which worked well for both of us. Doreen and her mother spent one Boxing Day with my family, and later I was to get to know her partner – indeed, for once I donned clerical garb when they asked me to bless their marriage. With the general manager's support I was finding opportunities to get involved in counselling in different ways than just as a therapist. As well as my plan for a counselling centre, I offered a paper I had delivered on optimism and pessimism in therapy and counselling to BAC, thinking it might help raise income for the association, and at the same time give me some kudos (Jacobs, 1980; revised and reprinted in Jacobs, 2009d: 53–73). I also edited the BAC referral directories in 1979 and again in 1981. However, we made the mistake of not consulting the management committee about the printing of my paper, and some of its members were very critical, partly I suspect because they saw me as using BAC for my own ends, which of course to some extent I was. But I was not the only one on the management committee with their own agenda, and I was aware that at times there were certain rivalries. Others also wanted to further their own interests.

The reader may get a sense of my role in BAC at that time if I extend my remark above that I am not generally a good committee member. I own up to preferring a leading role on a committee, or no role at all. The reason is a certain impatience with those who in my eyes are more interested dotting the i's and crossing the t's than in the bigger picture. I like to get things done, and if an idea – whether it is mine or someone else's – seems a good one, I get frustrated by any unnecessary delay. If I have achieved much in my career (such as the Leicester courses as well as all my writing), it is because I have largely got on with it without hindrance.

In Meredith Belbin's definitions of team roles, I am somewhere between a 'plant' and a 'shaper' (http://www.belbin.com/about/belbin-team-roles). The strengths of a 'plant' are creativity and solving problems in unconventional ways. A plant's weaknesses are ignoring incidentals and not always communicating effectively. That is definitely me! A 'shaper' is challenging, and thrives on pressure. But a shaper can be easily provoked, can sometimes offend people's feelings, and become aggressive and bad-humoured in the wish to get things done. That is also me. I am not a good team worker, nor am I a good completer-finisher when it comes to being a team member, although I am a good finisher when it comes to my own work. I am not much of a specialist, but I am, surprisingly, quite a good coordinator.

Up to the point of joining BAC's management committee, I always had been somebody who tended to work alone. This curious mixture of enjoying taking a leading role, and yet also enjoying being a backroom boy getting on with my own projects, has served me well. There have been few people with whom I have really hit it off in a creative working partnership. An exception had been at Sussex when Hugh Clegg and I found a mutual enthusiasm for a number of projects, including my becoming a counsellor. There was a similar enthusiasm in the way Doreen Schofield and I worked together, and a few years later I was to find the same with Moira Walker. In that last instance, our working relationship extended to marriage and probably the most creative period of my career.

To return to my narrative: Leslie Virgo, having asked me in 1978 to replace him on the management committee, rang me one day in 1980 to say that he wanted to propose me for chair of BAC at the coming AGM. This was again not something I had thought of for myself, and it seemed a massive jump from being a committee member. But Leslie thought I would get things done, and that I would be good for BAC. After I put the phone down, I had some misgivings about his proposal, since it had already become the practice, as in many organisations, that when the chair retires, the vice-chair takes over. The vice-chair and therefore the shoe-in to chair was Mary Godden, whom Leslie knew from his work in Kent. I was not at all sure about upsetting the apple cart, but I had always taken a lot of notice of Leslie, and his confidence in me prompted me to ring Audrey Newsome, the current chair, to see what she thought of his proposal. 'Leslie wants to propose me for chair,' I said. Audrey must have misheard me, because I think she heard me say 'vice-chair', or assumed that was what I meant. She responded enthusiastically, that it would be a very good idea to work alongside Mary. I did not have the courage to correct her and to repeat that it was as *chair* that Leslie was proposing me. So at the AGM held at Loughborough University in 1980, Mary (absolutely appropriately) was duly elected as chair and myself as vice-chair.

I had another idea that I wanted to put to the AGM. Concerned at the way unemployment was rising in 1980 under the new premiership of Margaret Thatcher, I talked over with Mary and Doreen beforehand a proposal for a conference on working with the unemployed. Both were enthusiastic and backed the idea. It would provide an opening for BAC to negotiate with government officials and other organisations for grants to enable a number of unemployed men and women to attend, and to engage speakers and delegates from other professions. The conference was organised remarkably rapidly and took place in July 1981 at Liverpool John Moores University. I presented a paper on the dynamics of being unemployed that was to become a major part of a chapter of the first edition of *The Presenting Past* (1985a: 172–85). I also edited the proceedings of the conference for another BAC publication (1981b).

The management committee had already approved of my plan to develop a voluntary counselling centre in Leicester. I saw it as a pilot project that BAC could use to promote and support the development of other such centres throughout the country, along the lines of the many branches of Marriage Guidance, although I think it may not have been seen that way in the minds of the management committee. While my own vision had developed from my visit to Oxford's Isis Centre, there were already other counselling centres such as Compass in Liverpool, and a developing network of WPF services. I hoped that if a pilot project was successful, BAC would be able to raise funding from government and other sources.

What the support of BAC actually amounted to was that the management committee agreed to pay for an initial mailing to interested parties in Leicester, which led to fifty people attending an inaugural meeting. Later the management committee, which had received regular reports from me, asked that a senior BAC member visit Leicester to assess how the project was working. Francesca Inskipp, who with Brigid Proctor had already done much for the development of training in counselling, visited and produced a positive report.

Since one purpose of the project was to encourage similar initiatives elsewhere, two papers were published in *Counselling*, one by Bernard Ratigan (1981: 5–9) and the other by Colin Lago (1981: 18–25). They were intended to be the first reports on the pilot. Bernard discussed issues of accreditation, training and supervision in setting up the centre. He recognised that the routes by which people had come into counselling were many, and that some carried more status than others. He referred to the third year of the 'embryonic counselling training' at Leicester University (see Chapter 5) and the possibility of a formal connection between it and the Leicester project. He acknowledged that there were opposing views on professionalism and elitism, and that qualifications from counselling courses were in themselves not an adequate licence to practise; although this was partly because trainings in social work, youth work, psychology and pastoral theology also addressed helping relationships. But he was prescient in raising the issue of whether BACP's registration of counsellors solely on the basis of having completed a BACP accredited course was in itself a guarantee of a licence to practise. It was also an important paper in respect of the accreditation of individuals and of counselling centres, which had not yet been undertaken by BAC.

In his paper Colin Lago, a counsellor at De Montfort University, discussed a survey of other counselling projects and how they had been initiated and developed. He had had a 62 per cent return on fifty-three questionnaires sent out to a variety of organisations listed in the 1978 BAC *Directory of Voluntary Counselling and Allied Services*. The information he received provides a picture of how counselling stood at that time. The organisations who responded had been founded from 1965 onwards, with many of them starting in the period 1974/75. Most projects had opened within one year of the birth of the idea. A whole range of professionals and backgrounds had been involved in the planning stage. Local authorities were seldom involved, although in some cases social services had played a part. Some organisations were developed to meet specific needs such as homeless girls, psychosexual counselling or unemployment. There were differences in what was offered, how often the projects were open, supervisory arrangements, and so on. Priorities in the early stages had been largely, as at Leicester, the training and supervision of counsellors.

The Leicester Counselling Centre opened in 1981 and is still going strong. The relationship with the courses at the university (see Chapter 5) grew and many students sought placements there, continuing to work as volunteers after they had qualified. In my time at Leicester there were as many as 100 voluntary counsellors with all the supervisors and receptionists acting in a voluntary capacity too. It became almost an accepted feature of the Leicester counselling and psychotherapy culture that when a trained counsellor or therapist moved into the area, or set up in practice, they were encouraged to give an hour or two a week *pro bono* to the work of the centre. At the time of writing, the centre still has over seventy volunteer counsellors, either fully qualified or in training.

The initial sponsorship provided by BAC faded and there was no progress on my original idea that the setting up of the centre could provide a model for BAC in initiating such centres elsewhere. That was perhaps partly my own fault, because I became much more interested in the local centre than in promoting possibilities elsewhere. But I have always regretted either that I did not do enough, or that there was never a similar enthusiasm for the idea in BAC. My perception of the direction that BAC was moving at that time was that it was becoming a vehicle for trainers to promote their courses (and their income) and for those in independent practice to legitimise their work. The voluntary element that had played such a part in bringing counselling into fruition was getting less attention with the push towards professionalisation. Looking back, I think this was one of the reasons why I was losing any enthusiasm for becoming chair when Mary Godden retired.

But before I took that decision there was another way in which I like to think I made an important contribution to the development of psychotherapy and counselling in Britain. In 1971, the Foster Report on Scientology led to the proposal that no one should be able to offer counselling or psychotherapy who was not accredited by a responsible body. A working party led by the barrister Paul Sieghart later presented proposals for the registration of psychotherapists at a meeting held in London on 30 July 1981 to consider his report. About thirty professional associations were invited to attend by the then Minister for Health, Dr Gerard Vaughan. The government's position was that the professionals needed to agree what they wished for by way of registration before the government was prepared to legislate.

I was asked to attend the meeting on behalf of BAC, after which I wrote a detailed report for the management committee, which was circulated for its meeting in October 1981. By chance I recently discovered that report in my filing cabinet, so can draw upon more than my fading memory of events all those years ago. I wrote about the different groups who spoke: the British Psychological Society counselled against registration; the British Association for Social Work was concerned for the protection of the public but not for the protection of the profession (which is what I suspect registration has actually become). The strongest support for registration came from the psychoanalytic and psychodynamic groups, while behaviour therapists voiced their scepticism about the need for a long training before registration, since research had shown that short-term training and short-term treatment were more successful.

I said in my report that there was general agreement that more research was needed into therapy abuse 'for greed or sex' and that a code of ethics was essential. The major disagreement was whether the standards required should be high and exclusive (this from the Tavistock) or lower and comprehensive to protect the public (the British Psychological Society). When I was asked to speak on behalf of BAC, I said that I could not represent the views of the association since the report had not yet been discussed there, but that BAC already had requirements that were stricter than in some other associations. I suggested that it was not sufficient to have a register of psychotherapists alone since the 'cowboys', of whom we might in BAC already have some, would then call themselves counsellors, making BAC into a dustbin. Paul Sieghart thought that counsellors only gave advice, although I was able to correct this impression afterwards in conversation with him.

However, there was no agreement over the need either for a further meeting or for a further working party. And that might have been the end of that, but by one of those accidents of fate. When we initially sat down I was seated next to my former therapist, whom I had not met with for some eight years and never outside his consulting room. We chatted before the meeting started, and after the meeting had finished he and I and a few other people who had been present were waiting at a bus stop outside the Elephant and Castle DHSS offices. Our respective buses must have taken a long time to arrive, because we discussed the meeting and agreed that we would have liked to have proceeded to a non-statutory council. I suggested to my companions that BAC, which they understood as similarly having a concern for standards, could host a residential meeting in Rugby, which being in the centre of England might make a convenient location.

On my return home, I consulted with Mary Godden and Doreen Schofield who both agreed to a weekend symposium on 16–17 January 1982 at Herbert Gray College, a meeting that Paul Sieghart agreed to attend as long as the different views were represented. With the agreement of the management committee, I met with three of the original bus-stop group. We arranged for two group facilitators from Nottingham University to lead the symposium, and sketched out the session times, leaving the actual form of the symposium to them. Given the short time frame, the BAC office set up the conference remarkably quickly and efficiently.

The weekend was a success. I only attended as an observer and to assist with the administration, with Mary Godden as chair representing BAC. I was not party to any of the discussions, nor did I have any say in the decision that there should be a follow-up symposium in January 1983. Thereafter I dropped out of any organisation of the follow-up, but the second meeting led to the setting up of the Rugby Conference and then to the Standing Conference for Psychotherapy. I don't know how it happened, but it appears that either BAC took the decision (after I had left) to cease to be a full member of the Standing Conference, or was forced by the psychotherapy organisations into the position of observer, along with the British Psychological

Society. The effect of the decision was regrettable, since it reinforced the division between counselling and psychotherapy, even though later both BAC and UKCP recognised that psychotherapy and counselling had a place in their respective organisations. BAC's *Therapy Today* has recently carried reports of closer liaison between the major therapy players, where BACP's place seems to be more fully recognised, but I often wonder whether that might not have happened all those years ago had BAC not allowed itself to be pushed onto the sidelines. Nevertheless, that first Rugby Conference stays with me as something of an achievement, even if it has long been forgotten how it came about, and even if BAC's active part in it probably goes unrecognised.

As I have indicated already, one of the reasons that led me to consider resigning as vice-chair – and indeed leaving BAC – was that I thought it was becoming an association for *counsellors* rather than an association for *counselling*. But there were other factors, some of which I may not have seen at the time. I was burning the candle at both ends: as the next two chapters show, I was heading up a rapidly expanding set of counselling courses, managing the university counselling service, supervising two placement counsellors, involved in some APCC responsibilities, and my first book was to be published in 1982, with further ideas for what I would write next.

I was also chairing the steering group that had recently opened the Leicester Counselling Centre, where the cooperation between leaders of the NHS psychotherapy unit, counsellors in two other local universities, the diocesan director of social responsibility, the Warden of Vaughan College (the university's adult education centre) and other interested non-counsellors contrasted with the lack of interest with which I felt BAC's management committee had towards my ideas for expanding counselling centres. It was promising to become the low-cost facility for local people that was close to my heart. The Leicester centre was already meeting greater demand than its first single counselling room could handle. It needed to take a risky step to expand significantly, yet had insufficient financial backing to guarantee that further expenditure would be matched by the necessary income.

And there were other factors. The general secretary of BAC and I had worked hand in glove for nearly two years, but she was leaving to get married and move to Scotland. I had always felt my ideas were welcomed and often acted upon by her, and I was not sure that I wanted to have to make a new working relationship with whoever might replace her. I suspect that she had favoured me at times, and that this had led to some tensions in the relationship between the two of us and the chair. For instance, I was asked to deliver the opening address at the inauguration of the Irish Association for Counselling in Dublin, whereas it should have been Mary Godden who fulfilled that function. I wonder too at this distance whether in having failed to follow through Leslie Virgo's desire that I stand for chair, that this led to my feeling that my capacity for producing ideas and for rapid decision-making which Leslie had recognised had clashed with Mary's more cautious leadership. Hers was probably the right way, but I felt sometimes frustrated by discussion when I wanted more action.

I was glad that a number of years later I was able to work again with Mary in a different capacity, although this time it was myself who was chairing a panel, the other two members of which were Mary Godden and Gabrielle Syme as past chairs of BAC. We met frequently for telephone conferences to review applications for membership of BACP by those who had a criminal record or who in some other way might be considered unsuitable for membership. This procedure was put in place following the humiliation suffered by BACP when the very non-PC comedian Bernard Manning applied for membership and was accepted. He had then exposed the inappropriateness of his membership in the gutter press. I was much older, and perhaps it made a difference that this time I was in the chair. We worked very well as a team, and made sound judgements upon what were on occasion questionable applications. Our panel of three functioned for a number of years before the decision was made to expand to several panels with constantly changing persons whom I did not know, which did not appeal to me.

But this was in the future, part of my second period of membership of BAC(P), which I describe in Chapter 7. I described myself earlier as someone who in teams is not a finisher. That is not altogether true in the case of my involvement with the Leicester Counselling Centre, but it is not true either of the way I developed counselling courses in Leicester, or of writing and editing, where I work quickly and always meet deadlines. These aspects of my professional life form the subject of the next two chapters.

Why did I not wait to become chair? Why in early 1982 did I resign not just from the management committee of BAC but also from BAC itself? I was only forty and very much flexing my wings having come through a fairly dark period when I first moved to Leicester. I had the sense that I might not fly so freely if I stayed. I am not really an organisational person, frustrated first by the Church and then frustrated by BAC. And even though I returned to BAC ten years later and valued much that BAC(P) did, I had and still have plenty of reasons to think that what had troubled me in those early years about the move towards professionalism and conformity was more and more borne out as regulations made it into yet another elitist organisation.

5

Developing opportunities for training

I have to step back a few years to open this new chapter in my professional career as a counsellor and therapist. One of the losses that I had experienced upon my move to the Leicester University Student Health Service was that my new role for a time effectively deprived me of ways of expressing a part of my nature that has always been important to me. Although Andrew Samuels, in a video we made on *Jung and the Post-Jungians*, describes me as an 'extraverted feeling type' ('feeling' in Jungian terms meaning 'reflective'), he only knew me at that point from my interviewing him in the studio (Samuels and Jacobs, 1995). In that video, he also makes it clear that there is also an introvert type in every extravert. I am a typical mixture of introvert and extravert, often a quite inward person and on occasion not always confident about putting myself forward. Another side of me, when I find myself in more public and social situations, can make a good fist of speaking with people, and I have little difficulty in encouraging people to talk about what most interests or concerns them, which is often themselves!

I had until ordination always been involved in acting in an amateur dramatic way, something I have often felt is the perfect way for introverted people to express themselves through adopting another persona on stage. Ordination and the priesthood brought with it a different type of acting. Being of the High Anglican persuasion, I liked ritual and the theatricality of the liturgy, and I could project myself well in preaching and lecturing. In my sermons at the University of Sussex, I liked to tackle difficult and meaty topics, which interested me and which I was told interested those who listened.

But in accepting my position as a therapist at Leicester, I had already agreed that I would not function as a priest. I could of course, as I did for a while, go to church, but I would not officiate at services. But as I have referred to earlier, after working as a university chaplain and listening to as well as delivering thoughtful and intellectual sermons, I found local church sermons were often dull and full of what seemed to me to be clichés. Going to church usually irritated me.

I no longer had any openings for teaching, as I had at Sussex where I had been involved in extra-mural education: co-facilitating classes that were less about religion and more about psychology and personal development. Suddenly I found myself in a nine-to-five job, shut up in my therapy room, enjoying the individual work, but feeling that another half of me was unable to find any outlet. At two points in my early years at Leicester I set up a small group that met at first in my home and then on neutral territory, where I gave talks based on the material I had been using in the extra-mural work at Sussex. They were moderately successful but there was no way of building on that limited opportunity. What I remember most about those groups was one of the participants who insisted on pronouncing 'Freud' as 'Fraud', though never disparagingly, however much I corrected him. Freud might have liked the Freudian slip.

Occasionally, but it was very occasionally, I had the chance to speak to a rather larger group. I remember addressing a conference of church workers on adoption counselling, about which I knew very little except through the experience of working with one pregnant student, and having adopted a daughter ourselves. But I relished the difference between that occasion and the more usual daily routine, and the next day, back in my office, I felt very low for a while. My only contacts outside the health centre to begin with were lunchtime breaks in the senior common room, and occasional attendance at APCC and ASC meetings.

About five years after moving to Leicester I was approached by Denis Rice, Warden of Vaughan College, which was the university's adult education centre situated above the remains of the Roman baths in the middle of the city. Despite being a Roman Catholic, Denis was responsible for the post-ordination training of Anglican clergy. He invited me to take a morning on pastoral counselling for his group. It was a lecture with questions, but it seemed to go down well, and I hoped I might be invited when he had a new cohort of recently ordained curates. Instead, in 1978, Denis invited me to teach a course on counselling as part of the university's adult education programme. It was to be for one term, just 12 two-hour sessions.

Although I jumped at the chance, I hadn't a single idea of what I would do. I knew that Alan Lilley, another priest who had changed career to become a student counsellor at Loughborough University, had been involved in counselling training, and I asked him whether he would like to teach with me. My own training at the Tavistock had been through lectures and group supervision, and I wanted to introduce a more practical element than I had ever experienced. I understood that Alan had previously used experiential exercises. I imagined that he could lead that part of each session, while I would take on the lecturing. As it turned out, once we got going we shared both aspects more equally.

There had been some clinical theology taught at Vaughan College in the past, and there was an existing module on transactional analysis. But generally in the country as a whole training for counselling had been limited to marriage guidance, and to a few universities such as Keele, Reading, Aston and Swansea that offered a year's full-time course mainly for school counsellors, as well as at least one part-time course led by Ellen Noonan in the University of London extra-mural department. During the 1970s, there was a surge of interest in counselling and psychotherapy training outside universities illustrated, for example, in the advertisements in BAC's *Counselling* in September 1980. The courses advertised were mainly in London (only four of the seventeen were not), and they covered a variety of modalities: transactional analysis, counselling in education, group analysis, Gestalt, psychosynthesis, pastoral counselling, psychodynamic counselling and transpersonal psychology. Only one of those courses was located in a university. Yet by the end of the 1980s, a large number of universities were teaching counselling as an extra-mural subject, and BAC was beginning to try to regulate courses through accrediting them.

Denis Rice was a group relations consultant and for a number of years had headed up an experiential course at Vaughan College on 'Authority and Role in Groups', along the lines of the Tavistock conferences on group relations held annually in the university's halls of residence, and where he had sometimes been one of the staff. I have already described the way in which those who had attended such courses (such as my own group training when I was a curate) spoke with each other as if they had been through a secret initiation rite, using esoteric language. There was therefore in some quarters in the city an awareness of and interest in matters psychological, which I suspect formed a basis for our new course.

We enrolled nineteen adult students. As such courses were measured in student hours, we contributed 456 student hours to the Department of Adult Education programme for 1978/79. We shared the lecturing and I started to design some experiential exercises to illustrate aspects of any topic when Alan had no previous material to draw upon. As I wrote in a paper ten years later, we taught most of what we knew in that one term (1990: 113–23). Ten years later, in September 1988, the new academic year started with myself working in the Department of Adult Education, with an office in Vaughan College, with twenty-four sessional tutors and over 450 students on a programme of thirty-five modules spread over the course of an academic year, both in Leicester and a second university centre in Northampton, amounting to a total of 16,500 student hours.

Those completing our one-term course said they wanted more, so we agreed that we would teach a further course the next academic year. We would repeat the course we had just taught, and then the two cohorts could come together for a module on counselling and personal development. We decided to use as textbooks an excellent study by my one-time therapist Eric Rayner (now in its fourth edition, 2005) and another by Gordon Lowe on the Erikson eight ages of man (1972). The latter came under considerable criticism because it was, as Erikson's stages tend to be, very male-centric, even to the cover, which showed several faces of a man from youth to old age.

The initial one-term course then became two terms, and the initial extension course similarly moved from one to two terms, and in time these courses were each spread over 34 two-hour sessions. Later, we added attendance on Denis's 'Authority and Role in Groups' as a compulsory subject, while courses such as the introduction to transactional analysis contributed to a growing set of optional modules. There were soon calls for a qualification of some kind, and we were able to provide 270 hours of teaching that comprised a basic certificate in counselling studies: the addition of 'studies' was to indicate that we did not consider the qualification sufficient in itself to become a counsellor, without further supervision and practical experience. But we did not want to deter those who wanted to use counselling skills in their own professional roles as social workers, teachers, nurses, clergy and even the occasional psychiatrist, from achieving a qualification that might further their career. All the courses were by today's standards very reasonably priced.

The issue of the number of hours training required to become a counsellor was even then on the horizon. Over a number of years I persuaded the Department of Adult Education that we were asking too much of students for a mere certificate. Certificates in other subjects required 360 hours of attendance and other lecturers agreed with me. Ultimately the department was able to change the counselling awards to a certificate in counselling studies (180 hours), an advanced certificate in counselling (a further 90 hours including supervised practice and 'Authority and Role in Groups'), and a non-graduate diploma in counselling (making a total of 360 hours in all). The awards for other subjects in the department were similarly changed. As the Leicester Counselling Centre expanded (see Chapter 4), students could apply for a placement there, which enabled many students to gain experience and to be assessed there on their practice.

Unfortunately, as far as I was concerned, the department's other certificates included three-hour examinations every year. Reluctantly, we realised we had to include that requirement too, wondering how to make an unseen examination relevant to training as a counsellor or in counselling skills. I convinced myself that the unseen element of an examination was like a counsellor not knowing what he or she would be presented with when meeting a new client. For the first examination, we decided that part of it would involve showing a film of a counselling session (one of which was Windy Dryden illustrating RET), asking the students to write critically and assess the method and Windy's practice. There was considerable comment about Windy devoting some care in his session to priming and lighting his pipe. We also showed Rogers working with Gloria. Eventually, I was able to change the examination process so that the students knew the questions beforehand and could prepare what they wanted to write. Then I dropped the formal examination altogether, replacing it with two essays that were set a few weeks beforehand and had to be submitted on a certain date in order to pass. I like to think that in teaching counselling we changed some of the educational practice of the department.

Following the marking of the examinations in the first and second years, I would initially see the students individually, whether or not I had taught them, to go through their papers. I remember after the very first examination that one student in her sixties had failed, because she had written very little on one of the questions. When I pointed this out, she replied that the instructions had asked for 'short notes on three of the following subjects'. She said that she had done as asked and written *short* notes! I offered her the chance of a re-sit, but she declined, saying she was too old to take exams, although she wanted to go on to the second course because it was such an interesting subject. In fact, she became one of the first counsellors at the Leicester Counselling Centre, selected because she possessed the skills although not an academic qualification; and she was a very effective counsellor for many years, a stalwart of the Centre in many different ways. It was another lesson to me, if I of all people needed one, that qualifications do not in themselves make a good therapist, and the absence of qualifications should not necessarily be a bar to becoming a counsellor, as long as the training is sound and the trainee's sensitivity and skills are obvious.

As the above figures suggest, the demand for places continued to grow, and I was asked to teach the course at the university's Northampton centre. To begin with, Alan and I taught a shortened version of the first-year course in the summer term, but with equal interest at that centre local sessional tutors were employed. I would always teach at least one module a year in Northampton. A full programme was offered, with Northampton students only having to travel to Leicester for the compulsory 'Authority and Role in Groups' module.

In 1978, there were nineteen students. In 1988, this had risen to 450 students. By 2002, three years after I had retired and an appointment had at last been made to replace me, there were over 800 students enrolled in Leicester, Northampton and elsewhere in the East Midlands, for the most part on the modular courses that could be taken over a period of years. Alan and I had begun to teach separately, each taking a co-tutor to train up, who in turn would take on their own co-tutor, so that sometimes the same module was available three or four different times in the week. The number and breadth of optional modules increased, offering much more than the psychodynamic model, and making possible ongoing training, now known as continuing professional development. Occasionally, a visitor from London would comment on such a diverse programme, wondering how these different modalities could sit so well together in the same programme. I always observed that in Leicester it was a question of using all the available good resources, and that it would increase our students' skills and knowledge if they were able to incorporate, if they so chose, approaches other than the psychodynamic.

One way of coping with the sheer numbers was to allow the size of the first-year classes to grow. Fortunately, we had in both university centres a large teaching space allowing for flexibility for small group or large group work. At one point we began to enrol fifty students for the first-year module with two tutors. About thirty of those would continue into the second year, but that was too large a dropout in the first year. When I lowered the numbers to forty, the dropout was much less, and the second year still tended to start with thirty. Such a large number had many advantages, particularly as my own books became available as course texts: lectures were largely replaced with preparatory home reading and discussion periods in class in small groups. Similarly, the use of experiential teaching meant that there were many more possibilities for students working with different members of the large group, even if divided into smaller groups, and always able to return to their fixed base group for part of the session.

I had realised by this time that it was possible to create imaginative exercises to demonstrate all manner of topics, to which some tutors added or substituted their own exercises. A two-hour session often consisted of discussions of the reading in base groups of six, staying the same throughout the year, experiential exercises and debriefing in groups which mixed people up, and reflection back in base groups. All the materials for the syllabus in the main modules were produced in tutor packs, together with overhead projector slides; and my role gradually changed to being an occasional visitor to the main modules to give the students a chance to give me feedback on their learning experience.

In order to further stem dropout from the first-year course, I introduced a ten-week module on counselling skills, taught almost completely experientially, using exercises developed and published in *Swift to Hear* (1985b). Later, I reproduced many more exercises from both main modules in *Insight and Experience* (1991). My hope was that these two books might encourage much greater use of experiential teaching elsewhere. While the micro-skills in *Swift to Hear* are fairly commonplace in one form or another in introductory counselling courses, the exercises in *Insight and Experience* (now out of print) illustrated various aspects of personality development and are mainly unique.

Micro-skills may be commonplace on counselling courses now, but many years after my own training at the

Tavistock Clinic I received an invitation from the tutor of the child psychotherapy course at the Tavistock to teach those skills over the course of a day. Her students had the opportunity to choose visiting lecturers from time to time, and someone in the group knew of my work through my teaching those skills in an induction day for clinical psychology students at Leicester. The morning at the Tavistock course went fairly well, with the students, now in their second year of training, commenting that no one had ever taught them such an analysis of listening and responding skills. They had only picked up how to be as a therapist from experiencing their own therapy and observing therapy through a one-way screen. They may have been enthusiastic, but their tutor looked rather sour, as if all this was beneath her. She sat aloof all morning. But during the afternoon, perhaps because she sensed that the experiential work was going down rather well with her group, she began to join in. It was a rewarding return to the establishment where I had trained so many years before.

Some of the exercises in *Insight and Experience* took place in small groups, but others used the large group. This was the advantage of working with a class of thirty to forty students. Since the book is no longer easily accessible, I will describe a few of the most interesting examples.

'A fictitious election' was designed to illustrate the dynamics of the shift from two-person to three-person relationships. Three participants, each one representing a different fictitious political party during the Commonwealth period in the seventeenth century (far from reality!), were provided with separate but balanced manifestos. They were supposedly in a situation where all three parties had won an equal number of parliamentary seats, so two parties would form a coalition and of those two one would appoint the first minister. I was astounded (although should I have been?) to find time and again that if there was one man and two women in the threesome, it was nearly always the man who achieved the highest office, and if not, it was seldom that the man was not in the coalition.

Another large group exercise in the second year came about by accident. Alan and I were teaching in Northampton, but there was one week when neither of us could be present. Instead of cancelling the session, we decided that we would not appear at all, and would leave the class to decide how it wanted to spend the evening. I based the idea on a talk I had heard years before by an American university chaplain, who spoke of an experiment he conducted with his student Christian community. One Sunday he deliberately stayed away from presiding at the mass, in order to see how the students would handle the situation with no priest present, since in his church only a priest was allowed to speak the most sacred part of the service. The students realised when he failed to appear that they were on their own, and after some discussion decided they would share out the service amongst themselves. One of them was asked to read the prayer of consecration – the most solemn point of the mass. But when they got to that prayer, the person nominated stopped and said that it didn't feel right to say it, since it was the priest's role. They then entered into further discussion, before deciding to recite the prayer in unison. It had been a very interesting exercise in looking at how people coped when the authority figure was absent.

How would our class cope if the two authority figures did not appear? They had had enough experience of working on their own, albeit with us there to set up exercises, call time, and provide some safety in case anything went wrong. But, and this was a big but, like the chaplain we would say nothing about our absence in advance. We would simply announce at the end of the session the week before that next week would be a rather different experience.

It was actually very difficult staying away. We each wondered how the class was getting on without us. When we returned the next week we received, quite appropriately, a very hostile reception, the more so when we revealed that we had done this intentionally. We might have broken their trust in us, because some people had felt so lost that the experience had not worked at all. When we tried to debrief their experience, it was clear that some had left early, and others did not want to talk about it – paying us back by themselves being uncooperative. It was a mistake, but we could still learn from it, without abandoning what seemed a useful idea completely. We decided to repeat the exercise the next year and to use it in Leicester too, but this time we would return to the class with about twenty minutes to go before it finished. That worked much better, since the anger was immediate, and we appeared in time to start unpacking the experience, a process that continued into the first half of the following session.

But it was still not right. What we needed to do was make it much clearer that the session was going to be different, and to find a way of observing and feeding back what took place. We therefore briefed the college staff to hand out instructions as the students arrived at the class at the start of that evening. Four out of every five were given a white sheet of paper with the words: 'This session is rather different. Some people have been asked to observe.' One in five participants was given instead a pink-coloured paper explaining they were not to join in, but to observe what happened as the session progressed, and suggesting a number of areas they might want to focus upon. We entered the room after the tea break with forty minutes still to run to the end of the session. We and other tutors (who bravely did the same as us) often found that the class had split into base groups as the safest place to be, but initially often had difficulty in deciding what to do with the time, as well as whether they should try to interact with other base groups. What became apparent was that those with the white paper instructions reacted against those with the pink sheets, seeing them as alternative authority figures whom they either ignored or were openly hostile towards, in one case labelling them as 'the pinkies'.

Now when we arrived there were a number of responses. Some individuals broke away from the groups that had formed, since they wanted to talk to the tutors straightaway. In other cases, some of the groups refused to join in the debriefing, because they wanted to carry on by themselves. There were variations in different years, and some good learning, but as time went on the exercise became pointless because gossip spread from year to year as to what would happen on the evening billed in the programme as 'Coping with the Unexpected'. They knew what to expect.

Another large-scale simulation was a session on adolescence. Briefing papers of different kinds were given to the students as they arrived, some for individual roles, some for roles in particular groups. The scenario was a wet lunch-hour when the fourth form (as it was in those days) had to stay in the school hall, with pop music provided for their entertainment. 'Teachers' were appointed from the class to oversee the hall, and the two tutors were present throughout. As the first half of the session wore on, these adult participants of different ages began shedding the years, walking like teenagers, slouching like teenagers, in some cases quarrelling with one another in role, or with another gang. They could be seen nudging and winking, for example as one of the 'boys' approached a group of 'girls'. After the break the 'teachers' took on the role of school counsellors to those with individual roles, before everyone was debriefed in their base groups. By the time they got to the role-plays, the individual 'adolescents' were truly deep into the part, making for a very effective counselling experience, but needing considerable debriefing.

The exercise that I liked most took place over the last two sessions of the second-year course. Base groups were given a short briefing on a new client coming for help, sketching in some background detail, and suggesting alternative responses to the client's first words. One of the suggested responses merited a higher score than the others; and one or two would score nothing or even a minus figure. Each group decided which of the suggested responses theirs would be, and delegated one of their number to check it with the tutors. The tutor would hear the response, inform them of their score, and provide them with the next part of the case material session, again with alternative responses. This format was repeated throughout the first teaching session and almost half way into the second. Inevitably the groups were excited if they scored positively, disappointed or even sometimes puzzled if they scored negatively. When the exercise was brought to a close, some groups might have a small positive score; some were however in the red. The reason for this was that time and again the 'best' response, which was taken from the one the original therapist had made, was not the most obvious one. Yet it had been right for that client in that piece of work. When it came to debriefing, we actually ignored the final scores, which had simply been a device to reflect the original client's battles of will with the therapist.

I relate this exercise in particular because its point was to show at the end of the two years of the certificate course that despite everything the students had learned, there are always responses which do not adhere strictly to the rules, responses that are not the most obvious ones, but responses which move the work forward. We wanted to show that standard responses as if from a manual are not sufficient and that each client and every situation is different. We were saying: 'You have learned much, but there is still much to learn. Don't always go by the book.' We wanted to show the value of the creative and some-times risky response, one that might find the right way forward with a client. For example, at one point in the scenario the client begins to talk more freely as the ses-sion is coming to an end: does the therapist stop as usual, or offer a further half-hour? In the original therapy, it was that extra half-hour that the therapist offered without it being asked for that had led to a breakthrough. The case was based on one of Masud Khan's called 'The Evil hand' (1983: 139–80). I was immensely appreciative when it came to publish the exercise in *Insight and Experience* that Khan's literary agent (Khan had died) gave permission to use the case in that way, replying that he thought Khan would have liked the exercise. I was similarly appreciative when Dr Meredith Belbin freely gave permission for me to publish my adaptation of one of his management exercises (Belbin, 1981), which I used to illustrate roles in an unstructured group.

What particularly interests me today is that the final exercise is reflected (but for quite the opposite purpose) in the Certificate of Proficiency that BACP now requires all aspiring members to take if they have not completed a BACP accredited course. The Certificate of Proficiency also starts with a few details of a first meeting with a new client, and provides a number of alternative responses, which similarly may score positively, neutrally or negatively. It likewise traces the progress of a piece of counselling work with alternative responses at every step. But my intention and the intention of BACP's admission procedure are diametrically different. The exercise I designed demonstrated the need for therapists and counsellors to work imaginatively, and not strictly to a set of rules, while of course staying within the boundaries of ethical practice. But the BACP exercise is designed to see if the candidate will say the thing that BACP wants them to say. When I followed the BACP's demonstration paper online, I found that some of the suggested responses that are positively scored are responses that I would hardly ever use, since I would regard them as intrusive and not client-centred. They follow a BACP agenda and not the client's. I find it ironical that the type of exercise I used to *challenge* standard responses is used for promoting standard responses in BACP's test of suitability for admission to their register. It is standardised responses that are scored positively. Had I taken the online paper I probably would have failed, and yet I would have done nothing unethical, and in my opinion would have better respected the client's agenda and needs!

In 1984, I was given a temporary contract (which lasted for some twelve years before it was made permanent!) as lecturer in the university's Department of Adult Education. I explain in Chapter 7 how this came about. The result was that it freed me to be able to develop the counselling course in ways I have described above, as well as giving me the time to write, as described in the next chapter. Moira Walker replaced me as head of the counselling service – again on a temporary contract. My concern in this book is with my professional career, not my personal life. But Moira's arrival, and her request that I supervise her work, led to my integrating her into our group of tutors, and later to our teaching together. We worked very well together and it became clear that our relationship could be more than a professional one. We stopped the supervision arrangement, but continued to teach together and I found myself even more creative in the different ideas I had. I have already portrayed myself as someone who has rarely worked with people who have really stimulated my creative potential, however much I had valued cooperative partnerships with people like Alan Lilley. But my partnership with Moira Walker, in both its personal and professional form, went on for twenty-five years until her death in 2013, a period in which she too led various initiatives and became an author in her own right.

We thought initially of developing a joint Centre for Counselling and Therapy in the university, linking the counselling service of which she was a far more dynamic head than I had been with the counselling programme for which I was solely responsible, since this would have enabled student placements in her service, and provided her staff with opportunities to teach. In fact this happened in a small way, but the finance department turned the plan down despite at first it being welcomed by a new vice-chancellor. It would apparently be too difficult to apportion the finances between the two activities of a joint enterprise!

Apart from teaching a main module together, we devised an optional course on therapeutic relationships, which became very popular. We not only examined the centrality and different dimensions of the relationship in counselling and therapy, but the therapeutic potential in other relationships, including work, friendships and partners. We based the course around some words of Harold Searles, writing about the supervisory relationship. Having suggested that he thought supervision was therapeutic for both supervisee and supervisor, he believed that *any* intense and prolonged human interaction could be mutually therapeutic – or anti-therapeutic (1986: 602–3).

We also taught an optional course on gender issues in counselling. We hoped to enrol twelve women and twelve men so that we could work experientially on a number of aspects of the subject. We advertised it in advance to the many students choosing optional modules, and the places for the twelve women filled within two weeks. But only one or two men enrolled. As the end of the term approached with our course starting the next, I asked all the tutors to inform their classes that there were still ten places for men, which we needed to fill to make the course work. These places then filled, albeit more slowly.

At the first session we asked the group what it was that had brought them to the course: what concerns were they bringing about gender issues? We divided the group into two, based on gender. In the feedback the women reeled off a long list of matters they hoped the course would address, which is why they had enrolled. The men said they had come because I had circulated a note asking for more men! It was like a call to arms! The second time we taught the course we abandoned the idea of a quota, and as is usual with counselling courses, there were more women than men.

Moira Walker taught her own courses on women in therapy, leading to a book with that title (1990) that I encouraged her to write; and she later introduced courses on working with survivors of abuse, an area in which she specialised. I began to teach a course from the books I had written on religion and illusion (see Chapter 6). I also developed a course on Oedipus, Hamlet and Ophelia, taking the lead from Freud's identification of Oedipus and Hamlet, but with gender imbalance in mind not wanting to neglect the fate of Ophelia. This was in the end to lead, after I had left Leicester, to a day workshop on Hamlet on the Couch and indirectly to my PhD (see Chapter 8).

Although the counselling programme was flourishing in Leicester, Northampton and further afield in courses that the university accredited, it had an inherent weakness. As the certificate, advanced certificate and diploma were structured, we could not comply with the requirements for BAC's scheme for the accreditation of courses that had come on stream from 1988. It was becoming obvious that some students who wanted to make a career of counselling needed to attend an accredited course. Some would start their basic training course with us, but then move to another university, even if it meant travelling, where their qualification would be recognised by BAC. I say something about the concerns some other university course leaders had about this, as well as myself, in Chapter 7.

But we failed to comply with BAC's requirements in a number of ways. We did not, for a start, select students. Anyone interested in training could enrol on the ten-week introductory course on counselling skills, run in parallel on two or three different days of the week each term. Those who wished to enrol for the first full-year course were not interviewed. For the ordinary certificate course there was no selection. This was important because the skills and knowledge which students learned were often of value to them in their work in teaching, social work, medicine and business. The only point at which selection took place was when students applied for placements as part of the advanced certificate. Most applied to the Leicester Counselling Centre, which had its own selection procedure that we trusted. From that point onwards reports were necessary, but experience suggested that those who had stayed the course and went on to placements had already selected themselves as suitable.

To illustrate the value of this approach, I could instance one student who was in a first- and second-year class that Moira and myself taught, who was very difficult, and caused her base group much trouble. She had been terribly abused as a child, and had spent many years sectioned in a mental hospital. She did not trust me at all, although she could relate to Moira. We had to work with her base group to help them function when she became difficult. Had there been selection I doubt very much whether she would have been accepted on the course, since we would have thought her too damaged; and had she come for selection for the second year, we would have thought her too disruptive. But as she progressed through the different stages, she settled, and with a huge effort she completed the diploma in counselling. She was named East Midlands Adult Learner of the Year. At the award ceremony she welcomed not just Moira but also myself, since I was becoming more acceptable and less threatening to her. She went on before she died to found a counselling service for abuse survivors, and she co-wrote a book with Moira. Leicester would have been the poorer without her, as indeed Leicester would have been poorer without the many hundreds of people who attended one or more of the counselling courses, and who took that learning into their work and personal relationships.

Another reason why we could not apply for BAC accreditation was that in the late 1980s I was the only full-time member of staff, and BAC required at least two full-time staff. At that time, to engage another full-time member of staff would put up the fees to a level that many could not have afforded. Our modules were remarkably cheap, but mainly because of low overheads. I secured agreement for a part time coordinator in Northampton, but that was not enough. Another requirement was for regular staff meetings that all the tutors attended. I had one such meeting a term but the sessional tutors had to come in their own time, initially without any extra pay.

Eventually Moira Walker wanted to move on from heading up the university counselling service, just as I had some years earlier. We were running a psychotherapy training together, and we realised that we had to offer a postgraduate diploma that could run alongside the existing programme, suitable for submission for BAC accreditation. It was agreed that the department would employ Moira part-time (later full-time) to run a programme that would meet BAC standards. It had limited numbers, although the number of students on our other courses continued as before. One entry requirement was to have completed the first-year module of the original programme or its equivalent elsewhere. The new diploma was indeed accredited after the first cohort had passed through, and it became a popular alternative, though with limited places.

We also wished to offer training in psychotherapy, an even more complex area to get accepted both by the university and the Standing Conference on Psychotherapy, who would need to recognise it. There was another recognised course in Leicester but only for those who worked in the NHS. We started by trying to get a postgraduate diploma of psychotherapy accepted by the university. The proposal had to be submitted to the Dean of the School of Medicine for his approval – and the Dean did not approve. Psychotherapy was in his opinion a medical discipline and we had no place in offering it. My own meeting with him was too confrontational (the reader will already be aware that I can get very impatient with authorities at times), although when Moira took over the liaison she seemed to get on quite well: she was at least invited to run a day on counselling skills each year for new intakes of medical students. But the Dean would not give way on the diploma. While she kept the Dean focused on what we knew would be a hopeless outcome, I went by another route, through adult education, proposing a non-graduate certificate in psychotherapy. It was the most we could expect, and it meant we didn't have to deal with the complications involved in an undergraduate or postgraduate degree. And what, after all, is in a name? The proposal went to Senate and was passed without the Dean of Medicine even being aware of it, so fixated was he on blocking the postgraduate route.

The course took twelve students every two years and recruited well, with trainees travelling long distances from the north, from Wales, from the east coast and indeed from London. I worked on three cohorts and enjoyed the opportunity to go into much greater depth with psychoanalytic theory and in studying significant psychoanalytic authors. While we only required a minimum of once-weekly therapy (and made it clear for that reason that our students should only offer the same frequency to clients as they had themselves experienced), we insisted on twice-weekly supervision in term time, once-weekly individual supervision in the area where they lived, and once-weekly supervision in a pair on the course itself. There was group therapy on the day of the course as well as their individual therapy. Because we had chosen the psychoanalytic and psychodynamic section of what became the UK Council for Psychotherapy rather than the Universities Psychotherapy and Counselling Association (see Chapter 7), we had to form a separate association for our graduates, since a university course could not register their graduates with UKCP except through UPCA. More complications!

This was a very innovative period, since we also introduced a certificate in psychodynamic supervision. To the best of my knowledge, no English university was offering any training in counselling and psychotherapy supervision in 1990, when we first had the idea of such a course. There were indeed few courses anywhere in supervision, although that is not the case today. We realised that it would not be possible to recruit sufficient participants in Leicester (although later I twice ran the first module of the course on a once-weekly basis for a small group of six). We therefore opted for a residential course, recruiting from the whole country, and as it turned out occasionally from abroad as well. We advertised a five-day residential at one of the Leicester University halls of residence, and rapidly filled the places.

When we first thought of the desirability of such a course, we had no clue as to what to teach on the syllabus. We just knew the number of sessions that would be available to us. We had never been trained ourselves as supervisors, although we had learned from our own experiences of being supervised and supervising what was helpful and what less so. That was a start, so we decided to open with that question: 'What has helped and what has hindered you in your experience of supervision?' We wanted the course to be experiential with some input from ourselves, as well as drawing on the experience (and inexperience) of those attending. The central core would be six sessions in which each one of a group of six engaged in a thirty-minute supervision with another member of the group. The four groups were to be facilitated by the two of us and two other experienced supervisors, whom we employed for those sessions. A vital part of those groups would be the feedback, which as facilitators we encouraged to be as honest as possible, demonstrating non-judgemental criticism.

We also decided that we could not subject anyone to this experience of supervising in front of a small group without subjecting ourselves to the same process, but in front of the large group. In the very first session one of us would supervise the other, asking the participants to analyse our work, and come back at us with the same honesty that we expected of them when they themselves were subject to scrutiny. There were also three sessions experientially demonstrating different types of group supervision. There were some lectures on the over-use of the concept of parallel process, on the games people play in supervision, and on diversity issues. We finished the course with a party at Moira's home on the last evening, and final sessions on the last morning of feedback on what had been learned.

The first course in July 1990 appeared to go well. It was a huge learning curve for both the two of us and the participants, especially when we began to observe and analyse each person in their role as 'supervisor'. Those core sessions never failed to be productive, especially when participants could give honest feedback. Only occasionally did this lead to a student feeling hurt, although it was fascinating to hear some of those then claiming that their mistakes were due to parallel process, despite my lecture on the over-use of the term.

Two features of the first course went less well. We were severely criticised by a few for the session on diversity, which at that time concentrated on gender issues. Moira and I knew how important gender was, since we had had to work on those ourselves when we first started working together. The critics thought that the whole subject was irrelevant and had no place on such a course. There was even a threat to complain to BAC! However, we did not change this session, but as the course developed we included all types of diversity as well as gender; and eventually the one session became two, with the participants breaking into small groups to reflect on the particular aspect of diversity they found most challenging, and the different groups presenting their ideas on working with issues of race, ethnicity, gender, sexuality, disability, and so on. The other complaint (and it seemed to come from the same people as the first) was that it was not right that we as tutors should have a party at Moira's home on the last evening of the course, because tutors should not mix in that way with students! Those remarks were hurtful, and for subsequent residentials we arranged instead for a meal together in an authentic Indian restaurant in Leicester. This was universally appreciated, and we would always go home at the end of that evening with plenty of doggy bags of curry for the freezer!

The success of the first conference led the next year to putting on two, followed by a second residential module, for sixteen students rather than twenty-four. The second involved working for much of the time on detailed analysis in groups of four of a tape of a live supervision session that each participant had to bring (with a transcript). We demonstrated more group supervision, looked at games that supervisors play, and engaged in other sessions that went at greater depth into the whole subject. The two residential modules provided the teaching component of the new certificate. The bulk of the remaining hours consisted of supervising and being supervised on that supervision in the student's own home area, a case study, a log and the submission of four hour-long tapes that were assessed with very detailed feedback. The annual five-day residentials became four (two of each), and knowing that we were going to move eventually to Dorset, we also conducted some residential courses in a former hunting lodge in a beautiful Dorset village, with students staying in B and B's, with all sessions and main meals in the main house.

Running parallel with all these developments was my writing, for which I am probably better known than anything else. The books speak for themselves, and there is no need to say any more about their content. But I believe that in some cases the story of how they came about, and some incidental information about writing them along the way, is of interest. What is particularly significant is that whereas my name may be associated with two or three bestseller texts, the books that have mattered to me most are those that have scarcely been noticed.

6

The right place, the right time

One of the curious experiences about being a fairly well known author (albeit in this narrow field of counselling and psychotherapy) is that many thousands (judging by the sales figures) know my books, but do not know me. At least they do not normally know what I look like. So if I attend some functions related to counselling, or even turn up to address a workshop, I either have to introduce myself, or if I am only a participant, I melt into the shadows unless there are people present who have met me previously. An example of what I mean was an occasion when I was speaking at a day conference. Taking coffee before the proceedings began, I noticed John Rowan across the room. I had co-authored *The Therapist's Use of Self* with him, and I was due to refer to that book in my lecture (Rowan and Jacobs, 2002). We had written the whole book through exchanges of emails, but I knew John by sight. I went up to him, tapped him on the shoulder, and cheerily said, 'Good morning, John'. He turned to me and said, in that rather forthright manner he sometimes has, 'Who are you?'

On another occasion I was waiting for a function to start and was introduced to someone, but only inasmuch as I lived in Leicester. 'Ah,' said the person whom I was meeting, 'Do you know Michael Jacobs who lives there?' I said I knew him quite well, since I was he.

I have been told by people who know me that I come across in my books as they perceive me, which is pleasing since when I write, I try to describe what I think and how I work as a therapist. I hope to be myself. I try to avoid terms and concepts that I do not myself understand, and I seek to communicate what I want to say in a rather ordinary way. I seldom write much that is original, and if I have anything to offer as a writer it is that I seem to be able to express in an accessible way what many distinguished psychotherapists and psychoanalysts have written before me.

I want to acknowledge at the outset of this chapter that I am somewhat hesitant about discussing books that in some cases have been very successful. I have no desire to make this an excuse for a sales pitch. I wish more to reflect on writing and editing books, which are in some cases known and in others little known in the counselling and therapy world. And if I have any gift for writing, I need to acknowledge that I have been fortunate in knowing the right people, and being in the right place at the right time. I would prefer the reader concentrate in what follows on the books and not on myself. Books have a life of their own, and when the manuscript leaves the author, others (editors and copy-editors) take it on, publishers own the copyright and they make the profit or the loss. As I write I happen to be reading the pseudonymous writer Elena Ferrante's *Neapolitan Quartet*, and I am impressed by her determination to keep her identity hidden. She apparently does not accept that her personal success can be measured by the success of her writing (Ferrante, 2016: 178).

Writing is a strange business. While much of it is indeed perspiration, much of it is also inspiration, and authors cannot, I believe, take personal credit for what develops once they let their minds run with a subject. Who knows where that inspiration comes from? Sometimes from what we know, sometimes from experience, sometimes from what we have read but can no longer attribute to an identifiable source, and sometimes from what we have forgotten we have ever read. At times we think we are being original, when in fact others have already said it before us. Elena Ferrante again puts it well when she suggests that in being creative we are to some extent taken over by others (2016: 59). This is so similar to the psychodynamic theory of our psyche being peopled by our interactions with significant others over our lifetime. I know that what I often do as I write is to express what I have absorbed and learned, but in my own way.

That certainly applies to the first article I had published. A few years after I had started as a counsellor and therapist in Leicester, and joined the Association of Pastoral Care and Counselling, I was asked if I would represent the association on the editorial board of *Contact*. This was a journal that had been founded by the Scottish Pastoral Association in the 1950s to promote pastoral studies. At the time I joined the board, it was sponsored by Frank Lake's Clinical Theology Association, the Institute of Religion and Medicine, the Westminster Pastoral Association (later WPF – the Westminster Pastoral Foundation) and the Irish Pastoral Association. I imagine I was asked because I lived in Leicester, nearer than most in APCC to Carlisle where the annual meeting of the board was held.

The meeting generally discussed recent issues, suggested ideas for future writing, and selected unsolicited contributions that might form a theme. Once I felt at ease amongst some rather illustrious names in the field of pastoral studies, I floated an idea which I would not mind working on, that had been suggesting itself to me from the medical setting in which I worked, but also from a novel I was reading and an evening class I was attending on ornithology. I was concerned about the way some referrals to me from one or two doctors came in the form of 'diagnoses' rather than the form of individual people – for example, 'I've got a very interesting obsessional compulsive I'd like you to see.' What felt novel to me at the time, although I realised later that it was not at all original, was that such labelling was de-humanising. Reading Ursula Le Guin's wonderful fantasy novel *A Wizard of Earthsea* (1971), attending the course on bird watching and a compelling question asked of me by a client about how I would classify her, led me to wonder if there was value in the concept of naming. I was in fact tackling a subject already in the air in the 1960s in the anti-psychiatry movement. But to me it was new, and perhaps to others it might have been new when my article was published in *Contact* in 1976. The article was later to form a major part of the second chapter in the first edition of *The Presenting Past* (1985a), a chapter added to and subtracted from in later editions; and in a revised form I included it in my collected papers *Our Desire of Unrest* (2009c: 33–51).

It was at those Carlisle board meetings that I first met Frank Lake, of whom I had heard much when I was a curate. We would travel back together on the train to Crewe where he changed for Nottingham, while I went on to Nuneaton to change for Leicester. Frank would talk nineteen to the dozen throughout the journey, so much so that I wondered what he was like as a therapist. He was a remarkably quick thinker, although he tended to pick up ideas and run with them without really working out their full implications. This included new approaches to therapy, such as LSD as a way of reaching back into infantile memories, although he later preferred deep breathing to achieve the same end. At that time he was into Janov's primal scream therapy, and he would recount stories of his successes with weekend groups using that approach. I remember vividly how he enthused about one participant who on the last afternoon of a weekend's primal screaming had had such a powerful experience that he exclaimed, 'I must have another primal'. That for Frank was sufficient evidence of the effectiveness of this new therapy.

I'm afraid my association to his patient's response was that it sounded like 'I must have another orgasm'.

Frank would always leave the carriage saying 'Thank you for listening', so I must have served some purpose. And it may have been my willingness to attend to him that resulted in a telephone call in 1978 from John Todd of the publishers Darton, Longman and Todd. DLT had published Frank's massive tome *Clinical Theology* (1966), which, when I mentioned it to Eric Rayner my therapist, he said was 'neither clinical nor theology'. But many clerical and lay pastors in the late 1960s had been trained using it, or through the earlier papers that had been published in it. John Todd had received a manuscript for a second book from Frank, and he wondered whether I would read the manuscript to see if it was worth considering for publication. I think Frank must have suggested me as a reviewer. When submitting a proposal, an author is sometimes asked for suggestions as to who might review it.

A weighty parcel arrived, consisting of about 600 pages, some closely typed, some dog-eared, some printed papers he had given at conferences, some slices of text pasted to the page. He proposed the title *Tight Corners in Pastoral Counselling*. It was a huge task to read through it all. I realised quite quickly that there were some gems in those pages, but a considerable amount of waffle and unintelligible theory, at least to the average pastoral counsellor not trained in clinical theology. It was like the spilling out of words that I already knew from my train journeys with Frank. But I thought there might be a useful book there, although as I told John Todd, the manuscript would need drastic editing, cut down to about one-third of its size.

This was fed back to Frank, and DLT came back to me. Frank would agree to the editing, but he wanted me to do it. I said I would on the one condition that Frank was to have nothing more to do with it, but leave it to me to present the publisher with what I thought might make a good book. Frank agreed. So began the even harder task of distilling what I thought was the wisdom of his experience, cutting out much that to my mind would not be of any relevance to the average reader, and might even be off-putting to the majority of pastoral counsellors. My literally blue pencil slashed through the pages. I found myself able to write link passages and sometimes even adapt or re-write what Frank had written, remarkably as it seems to me, in his own style. It was, or it could have been, a seamless work.

Alas, there's many a slip . . . The page proofs had to go back to Frank to read and correct, as well as to myself, and Frank insisted on inserting a number of extensive footnotes and a new long preface, which together largely restored some of the very material I had cut out. To my mind he had spoiled the chances of the book making a positive impact, although I did not know any of this until the finished bound book arrived as a complimentary copy. I was not alone in my reaction: a review of it in *Contact* by Professor Alistair Campbell was very critical. This might have reflected on me, although thankfully Frank had only made a brief reference to my part in the book.

I was by then associate editor of *Contact*, and I learned from the editor David Lyall that Frank had reacted very badly to the review. He had written a stinging response that he insisted was printed in the journal. As Frank was a member of the board David felt he should include it, although he was unhappy about an author responding to a bad review, as I have always been. I have occasionally felt misjudged or misunderstood in a review, but have always resisted the temptation to pen a reply. Publishers say a bad review is better than no review. I am not so sure.

It was known, and Frank knew, that he was dying when he had written his response. We wondered whether he knew he would not see any reply to his protest. Nevertheless there was: Alistair Campbell penned a sensitive letter that appeared in *Contact* after Frank had died, which opened with the words, 'Dear Frank in heaven . . .'

I wrote several more articles for *Contact* over the years, many of which were eventually included in *Our Desire of Unrest* (2009a). I also had the task as assistant editor of writing abstracts of articles from the *American Journal of Pastoral Care*. The United States had and has a much stronger and well-established tradition of pastoral care and counselling, and I gained much from reading their journal. It was in one of those articles that I first recognised the value of identifying what are now known as the micro-skills of the counselling process. Drawing upon them, and adding to them, I later developed the introductory course on counselling skills that fed into the certificate and diploma programme referred to in Chapter 5; and from that course published *Swift to Hear* (1985b).

As a result of being on the board of *Contact* in APCC I proposed, and volunteered to edit, a newsletter for the association, where a Catholic priest and an RAF chaplain joined me in the task. This meant that I wrote short pieces and reports, and managed the book reviews section of the newsletter. I was therefore able to solicit books for review, which added to my reading. I got to know who was and who was not a good reviewer for other books – good being someone who delivered their review on time when asked to. The network of contacts I was building up amongst counsellors and others was useful when I was looking for contributors to books I later edited.

Perhaps it was as a result of my contributions to the newsletter as well as my article in *Contact* that Derek Blows, then the director of WPF, asked me to write a volume on pastoral counselling in the *New Library of Pastoral Care* of which he was to be the series editor. I was by then teaching the course at Vaughan College (see Chapter 5) and so already had an outline of the book in mind from the lectures I had delivered. I intended to write an accessible, non-technical introduction to the psychodynamic process.

Those who now work in university counselling services will no doubt be envious of my situation at the end of the 1970s. Although I had a very full caseload during much of the academic year, it was only in the ten weeks of the three terms, and even then it went down over the examination period in May and early June. The vacations were fairly slack. I was able to write the book over one long vacation, and I sent it to the editor for approval. Derek came back at me with a number of criticisms, which suggested I might need to re-write some of it. This was before word processors, so re-writing meant having to type it all out again from scratch, at least if you wanted to present the publisher with a neat copy. In my case, I had sent my rather badly typed scripts for re-typing to a retired secretary who also typed the APCC newsletter. Any request to re-write was a real chore. It has been very different since the advent of the word processor, where the temptation is the opposite one of fine-tuning a script *ad infinitum*.

I pointed out to Derek that I had followed precisely the outline I had given him in the first instance. He had agreed to it, so why did I need to alter it? He relented, and the book went ahead. I suspect that one of his qualms was that I had really not addressed the theological and spiritual issues that are raised by counselling in a church context. Indeed, the chapter in the book that is called 'Beliefs and values' posed me with a problem. I had many doubts about much of the teaching of the Church, about the use of prayer in counselling, and the projections people made on to divine figures. I wanted to address some of the very concerns that made me cautious in my practice about getting into theological and spiritual issues in therapy. I wanted the book to be one we could use on our counselling course, which had some clergy and Christians on it, but many of no obvious faith as well. I looked therefore at the need for openness to different beliefs, at the need to temper convictions that clashed with a client's, or where necessary to own to them, so that a client could choose whether or not to engage with the pastoral counsellor. I discussed some of Freud's objections to religious belief, and I included a long example of how to handle requests for prayer, taken not from my own practice, but from an article in the *American Journal of Pastoral Care.*

I must have done something right. The book did not appear to worry most of those critical of religion, and appeared to go down well with students on the course. Curiously, I began to have a few evangelical Christian students come to me for counselling, believing that because my book was published by a religious publishing house, I must be a Christian. This was quite a contrast to the time that I have already referred to (Chapter 2) when I was a chaplain at Sussex University, where I always failed to pass muster.

I had wondered about the right title for this, my first book. I wanted a title that caught the eye – not simply 'An Introduction to Pastoral Counselling'. I remember the time and even the place when the words 'still small voice' flashed into my mind. I was driving back late one morning from a BAC meeting in Rugby on the then A50 between Husbands Bosworth and Leicester. Not that it was like Saul, a conversion experience, but it illustrates what I mean by 'inspiration'. The phrase was from the Old Testament story of Elijah in the 1611 translation, and appears in the hymn 'Dear Lord and Father of mankind': after the wind, the earthquake and the fire, the 'still small voice of calm'. The title seemed to encapsulate both the necessary stillness of the counsellor, and the hope of calm for the client in place of intense emotional distress.

It was a good title, and the book caught on. It sold 3000 copies in the first full year of publication and, slightly changed for a second edition in 1994, it continued to sell. Remarkably it is still in print, now with a trickle of sales, after nearly forty years. The three-word title encouraged me to seek, sometimes mistakenly, for similar catchy titles for later books. *Swift to Hear* (1985b) and *Holding in Trust* (1989), both phrases from the New Testament, were later titles in SPCK's pastoral care series. It could easily have been a mistake to use the title *The Presenting Past*. When John Skelton of the Open University Press took the book he was not at all sure it would sell, because he thought it appeared to be about archaeology, not psychology.

Flushed by what seemed like success (limited of course compared with real bestsellers) I started work on a companion volume, to include the lectures I was giving in our second-year counselling course. Having a book which covered the material in those lectures would mean that students could read a chapter a week as home study, making much more time in class for discussion and practical exercises. But I should have realised that publishing is a strange world. When I offered it to SPCK, their response was that it was not relevant to their list. I was stumped, and sought advice from Ellen Noonan, director of the counselling course at Birkbeck College, University of London, and the author of a very good book on working with adolescents (1983). She suggested, although it was not her publisher, that I approach Harper & Row, to whom I duly sent the manuscript.

I must have had an acknowledgement, telling me they would let me know, but otherwise I heard nothing for months. I waited and waited, and in the meantime started on a second proposal (*Swift to Hear*) for SPCK, a prequel to *Still Small Voice* (1982). It was my third book in the order of writing, but I waited for so long for a response to *The Presenting Past* that it actually appeared as my second.

That might have been the end of the story. When eventually *The Presenting Past* was published, in January 1986 (misleadingly dated 1985), it went nowhere. It only sold 700 copies in its first two years. It was Windy Dryden who was partially responsible for rescuing it. Rupert Murdoch was to buy Harper & Row to turn it into the imprint Harper-Collins. Windy, entrepreneur par excellence, although at that time fairly unknown outside rational-emotive therapy circles and Aston University, wrote to all the authors on the

Harper & Row counselling and psychology list, expressing concern at the Murdoch takeover and offering to take the list elsewhere. I don't know how many of us agreed, but I had nothing to lose. The rights were sold to the Open University Press, at that time still under the wing of the Open University. Despite what their managing director John Skelton later told me about the title, remarkably the fortune of the book completely changed. And it was the start of the most fruitful of relationships with that publishing house, leading to a sequence of books I either wrote or edited, which to date amounts, including this one, to forty-two volumes in all.

Any reputation I have as a writer really owes much to Windy Dryden, himself currently the author and editor of over 200 books, and emeritus professor of psychotherapeutic studies at Goldsmiths College, London. Conceiving the brilliant idea of the series *Counselling in Action* with Sage Publications, he commissioned the first four volumes on feminist, person-centred, cognitive-behavioural and psychodynamic counselling, all published together in 1988. His brief to his authors was simple, to describe the process of counselling from beginning to end.

I think I was the only one to take him at his word, by choosing to describe work with two clients from the first session to the last, tracing the counselling through the various chapters. I had in my earlier books used case vignettes suitably disguised, so well disguised that two of my clients who read *The Presenting Past* wondered why they were not in it. They were! In the first edition of *Still Small Voice*, I also used brief anonymous examples, but I wanted to finish with a longer case example in which I revealed details of the client. The counselling had ended, but I got in touch and asked her permission to use the example, which even in its disguise would have been obvious to her (and her alone). I later made the mistake of updating the example in the second edition of that book, without again seeking her permission for the change, since I assumed mistakenly that

I was not adding anything that went beyond the already disguised details. The former client was furious with me, although we met and talked it through, and she accepted my apology. I hope I am forgiven.

When I started to write *Psychodynamic Counselling in Action* (1988), I knew it would be impossible to use actual clients right through the book. I toyed with the idea of drawing upon fictional characters, initially seeking inspiration in Graham Greene's novels, but soon recognised that this raised copyright problems however much I adapted his characters and their situations. I was reading a lot of Dickens at the time, and so I drew upon *The Old Curiosity Shop* and Little Nell for the first client Hannah, and upon *A Tale of Two Cities* and Dr Manette for the second client Karl. The names I chose for them was a way of paying a kind of homage to Anna Freud and Hannah Segal (Klein's major interpreter), and Carl Rogers and Carl Jung, for no other reason than that they were significant figures in the field, although not in the latter case a huge influence on me.

As the preface to the book now explains, I had intended that my work with the fictional Hannah would be an example of counselling that went well; and with Karl of counselling that presented problems and yielded limited results. It is too glib to suggest counselling always works well. It was my only attempt ever to write a type of fiction, drawing of course on my experience of a variety of actual situations, just as novelists inevitably draw upon their perceptions of people they have met or known. Strangely, as the book proceeded, although on the whole things went well with Hannah as I intended, she left prematurely without any sense that we had resolved any of her issues. And while things were very difficult with Karl, it ended well, even if due more to the accident of time and events than through anything particular that I had done or said. The characters had taken me over, and refused to be manipulated into any other ending than those that Dickens had given them.

I think the device worked, even though I heard that one psychodynamic course refused to use the book because the case examples were fictional. It may also have been because I was not psychoanalytic enough for their taste. Much though psychoanalysis has taught me, influenced me and earned my respect, I prefer to practise and write about a version that merits the title 'psychodynamic' rather than 'psychoanalytic'. I believe it is more relevant to the once-weekly work of most counsellors and many therapists. Now in its fifth edition, the book has changed considerably as the years have passed, in the same way as my practice has mellowed from what I thought I had to represent when I first wrote the book. It remains my single most successful publication. With the decline in counselling courses, upon which I reflect in Chapter 8, sales are falling off. But I am sometimes amazed that thirty years after it first appeared, the book can still prove useful.

Windy Dryden is a superb editor, although he has told me that he does not have to do much editing on what I write for him. He designs the outline of a series well, with clear indications for his authors about their book's structure. He drew initially upon those of us who were pioneers in the counselling field for chapters in the various books he was editing, and for his second major series on *Key Figures in Counselling and Psychotherapy*. He has done a great service for the counselling world. He has also been one of the most broad-minded of therapists, however much he is wedded to what started, when I first knew him, as rational-emotive therapy, which morphed into rational-emotive-behavioural therapy and yet again to rational-emotive-cognitive-behavioural therapy! How long I wonder before he adds 'psychodynamic'?

Windy asked me to write the Freud volume for his second major series. This meant considerable study of Freud in order to ensure that I gave as accurate a picture as I could, although looking back after many more years of reading Freud and about Freud I realise that the subject is inexhaustible. I would have a hard job today producing such a slim and measured volume. A couple of years after *Sigmund Freud* (1992a), Windy asked me whether I would take over the title on Winnicott (1995b) since the original author he had in mind was unable to do it. That person would have been much better placed than me to undertake the book, as his subsequent publications on Winnicott have shown.

Writing the Winnicott book involved even more research than the Freud volume had. Apart from reading his published work, which I had not done in much detail before, I wanted to talk to those who knew him and worked with him. Unlike in my research for the book on Freud, some of Winnicott's former colleagues in Britain were still alive. I received enormous help from everyone I approached, from Nina Farhi and the Squiggle Foundation, from one of his former paediatric registrars, and from others I consulted by letter and in person. I was privileged to be invited to a reception at the Freud Museum on the hundredth anniversary of Winnicott's birth, and there was introduced to the very old, very gracious *grand-dame* of them all, Marion Milner, whose work I also admired. While the Winnicott book has not gone as well as the one on Freud, writing it was a much richer personal experience.

Having published with both Sage and the Open University Press, I found myself the object of competition between them for one series. I had had the idea of a series which would attempt to identify and cluster parallel concepts in different therapies: different terms in various modalities are sometimes used for the same concepts, even if there were clear differences between them in other respects. At the same point at which I put my proposal to Open University Press, Sage was interested in a very similar idea of Ray Woolfe's, a counselling psychologist whom I had met when serving on a British Psychological Society working party. Sage approached me saying that Ray did not himself want to edit the series but was happy for me to do so. So I had two commissioning editors, with each of whom I had published, wanting me to edit a series that, to all intents and purposes, would be pretty much the same.

So started a short bidding war, which I found both difficult and somewhat distasteful. Sage offered me more royalties than Open University Press. Open University Press came back with a better offer. Sage upped theirs. But by this time I did not want to be involved in a tug of war in which I was the rope, and I went with the publishers to whom I had myself first broached the idea, Open University Press. This meant that Ray Woolfe never received the recognition he deserved for his idea. But perhaps it is better that there were not, as there might have been had he chosen to edit Sage's, two identical competing series.

I wanted the series to be multi-modal, multi-national and gender-balanced in its selection of authors. Being the late 1990s, I was able to cast the net wide online for possible contributors. The Internet was becoming more widely used and I had joined a psychology forum where various issues and questions of practice were debated. I floated the ideas I had on the forum asking for therapists to get in touch if they were interested. Although the actual elements of the series had not been decided, I wanted each volume to be authored by two authors of different orientations, and living where possible in different parts of the world. I hoped for as many women respondents as men.

It was a tall order, but the offers came in, and somewhat blind as to their abilities to write I selected a representative group. I persuaded the Open University Press to pay for a 24-hour residential conference of the likely authors at Launde Abbey in Leicestershire to design the series. I imagined that only those living in Britain would attend, although one American contributor flew in at his own expense to join us. As a result of our discussions, fourteen topics were identified, which seemed to cover the various theories and practices of psychotherapy. We began to identify who might be best suited for each topic, and whom that person might be twinned with. The two authors in each volume would communicate by email, their chapters going back and forth between them, with myself as series editor copied in each time. At first this was fairly straight-forward, and contracts were issued.

What is remarkable and gratifying is that on the whole the original plan worked out well. Several of the volumes had pairs of authors living on different continents, and even more had at least one author who was not British. In the end, of the twenty-five contributors to the four-teen volumes, five were from the United States, one from Canada, three from Australia and two from South Africa, although when we started there were others from Europe and Israel. Initially I also had a fairly good balance of men and women, although rather more women than men had to drop out because of pressure of work. Most of the volumes were written as originally intended by authors from dif-ferent orientations and work settings, although a few had two authors who knew each other and worked in a simi-lar way, but who researched other modalities thoroughly. The final line-up included clinical psychologists, child and adult psychoanalysts, a cognitive-analytic therapist, transpersonal, person-centred, psychodynamic, Adlerian, humanistic, holistic, embodied-relational and integrative therapists, psychiatrists, a residential social worker and a psychiatric social worker, and others working as coun-sellors and therapists with families, couples, in university counselling services, private practice, and so on. Of the twenty-five authors, nine were women.

I had not planned myself to write for the series, since editing some authors is as arduous a task as writing, espe-cially when working with those who have not published before. Early on I stepped in to pair with John Rowan on what has become one of the most popular books in the series, *The Therapist's Use of Self* (2002). I was happy to work with John's outline for the book, and our exchange of views, including agreements and disagreements, went smoothly. As two experienced authors we wrote well together.

In two of the other books, one author dropped out before contributing much, while the other had taken the lead and had already produced considerable material. It was easier for me to step in as a second rather nominal author, where I only acted in my editorial role, contributing occasionally, but never writing anything substantial. Between 2001 and 2007, the fourteen different volumes were published, with varying degrees of success.

A near disastrous error occurred in one of the email exchanges after I had received copy from each author on one of the volumes. They lived in different countries, had different orientations but they were getting on really well personally. But as I read the sections they were each writing, their writing styles were very different. One was more measured and formal, the other more chatty and informal. This may have reflected how they were as therapists and indeed their orientations, but such completely different styles would not work. I wrote an email to the one who was more in line with what I had in mind, saying that I was not happy with the other's style, and wondering whether he might undertake the final polish in order to align the two styles. My error (or was it a Freudian slip?) was to inadvertently copy the second author into the email. His immediate reaction was understandable: he was hurt and angry and I nearly lost him. I am glad to say he stayed with it, and the resultant book, thanks to both of them, is very good.

The task of editing the series was the largest and longest project I have undertaken. Editing some authors was straightforward, but others required some re-writing, which at times was easier to do myself. I had retired early from the University of Leicester in 2000, doing a little teaching and with a small therapy practice, so I had more time to devote to the task. When still at the university I always set aside one day a week purely for writing and editing.

Even then, as many writers will know, it was (and is) easy to fritter away the time by doing anything but: answering letters, catching up on emails, and generally clearing the desk of a week's outstanding tasks. I wonder in my own case whether this is because when I do start (and it may take one or two hours) I find it impossible to stop, and tap away on the word processor resenting anything that interrupts me, including meals.

If *Core Concepts in Therapy* was a large project, the 1990s was my most productive period as a writer. I was also working for the Open University Press to oversee proposals for their counselling and psychotherapy list, including developing two series with Moira Walker as co-editor. Moira proposed a series on how counselling worked in different contexts: in social work or medical settings, with women, with young people, in independent practice, etc. There were eventually twelve volumes in all, which we divided between us for editing.

I proposed a series on how different therapists might work with a particular client, where Moira and I each took on two books, while I later worked on a fifth on supervision. If *Core Concepts in Therapy* had the potentiality to make an important contribution to identifying similarities and differences between the modalities at a theoretical level, this earlier series, *In Search of a Therapist*, had a similar function in relation to differences in practice. It took real situations and looked at how therapists from different modalities actually worked, and how they differed in the way they understood a client.

My project was for four sets of six therapists to discuss how they might work, each set with a single client. It had been done before, but with fictional clients and with only six therapists, whereas I had in mind four actual clients and twenty-four different modalities. I toyed with a title for the series that mirrored Pirandello's play *Six Characters in Search of an Author*, but eventually settled on *In Search of a Therapist*. In the event it might have been better to be less clever, with a clearer title such as *Comparing Therapies*, because the main titles of the four books became the pseudonyms of the four clients – *Charlie, Peta, Morag* and *Jitendra*. A fifth volume, *In Search of Supervision*, has a much more obvious title, which perhaps is one of the reasons it has sold relatively well.

Each book in the original four worked this way: Moira and I were responsible for two clients each. We met each one for an hour, facilitating them in saying what they sought from therapy and why, but with minimal prompting from ourselves. A transcription of the hour would be sent to six therapists from different modalities, who then had the opportunity to ask clarifying questions, or to set certain tasks for the client, such as to enact their situation in a drama, engage in a guided fantasy, or complete a psychometric test, according to the practice of each therapist. Having collated these questions and exercises we worked through them with the client, without identifying who the therapists were or what their orientation was. This resulted in a series of meetings with each client that were recorded and transcribed, and the separate questions were returned to the particular therapists who had asked them.

The therapists worked on the material they had asked for, formulated how they understood the client, how they would want to work with the client, and how they foresaw the course of therapy. Each contribution was sent to the client, and finally we met with each client for one or two hours to gauge their reactions, and see whether they could identify which of the six therapists would be most suitable for them. We wrote up the final chapter and sent it to all the parties before publication.

There were clearly ethical questions here. We could not use someone who was already a client, because that would interfere with their therapy. We did not want to use anyone who had been in therapy, since that person would already have been influenced by the therapy they had already received. We wanted clients who had never had any counselling or therapy, who were willing to be open. We would disguise names and any identifying features. We made it clear to volunteers that we could not ourselves work with them, apart from in the way I have described, and that even when the process was complete, we could not offer them therapy. If they then wished, we would help them find a therapist. In the meantime, over the months that the process took, we did not want them to engage in any other therapy, and of course we wanted them to stay the course.

We declined some who had volunteered, since they had presenting issues that were potentially too serious or they were not robust enough. At first we selected three, but they were all women. We wrote to various therapists we knew or knew of, and selected twenty-four in total, all of different modalities, and divided them into groups of six, trying to mix them as far as possible, so that any that might be slightly similar (variations on psychodynamic, for instance) were not in the same group. It was a very smooth process. However, I wanted a male client, and I had hoped in the multi-cultural city that is Leicester that someone from a different culture would have come forward. Since none volunteered, I had to ask someone I knew whether he would be interested, and so I was able to proceed with the fourth volume.

It was a remarkable experience for these clients and for us. I think it is fair to say that it was for them a therapeutic experience, which ranged from being simply worthwhile to opening up very positive possibilities. With each client we shared in learning a great amount about how different therapists might work. Much could be said about the way in which our clients responded to the six therapists, but it is recorded in the final chapter of each book. There were, however, two experiences that deserve separate mention.

The first was with the client we called Charlie (Jacobs, 1995a). One of her six therapists was Tony Ryle, who set tasks for her that form part of cognitive-analytic therapy.

What impressed both Charlie and myself was his initial letter to her, which is part of the CAT process, although in his case it was only based upon the initial transcript and the further information he requested. I read this to her in one of the follow-up sessions and gave her a copy. It was a remarkably sensitive and perceptive piece, which really moved her. Since I knew Tony and had worked with him many years before, I recognised it as a mark of his skill and perceptiveness and of his long experience.

The second example that particularly impressed me was with Jitendra (Jacobs, 1996b). I had received back five of the final contributions, and was despairing of whether the sixth would ever appear. I had to proceed to the final stage, and I went through the five contributions with him. When we came to the end of the process, believing that the sixth contribution was going to have to be dropped, I asked Jitendra which of the five therapists he would want to work with if he had the opportunity. He singled out one contribution by a woman therapist, which was indeed perceptive. I could see how it might appeal to him, since it included aspects that were in accord with his cultural background. The sixth eventually arrived very late, but before going to press I sent it to Jitendra and we met again. Without the sixth therapist knowing anything about the other contributions, or what had happened in the final session I had had with Jitendra, his chapter suggested that he thought Jitendra would choose to go with a certain type of therapist, who would fit Jitendra's fantasy of an idealised woman. He accurately described the type of therapist whom Jitendra had chosen and indeed had idealised in our concluding interviews. It was another instance of the real perception a therapist can have of a client, even at a distance.

Perhaps the most personally testing of the books in the series was *In Search of Supervision* (Jacobs, 1996a). Setting up the project presented tricky issues. I had to find a client with whom it was possible to record a session and submit a transcription to six supervisors from different modalities. For much of my career I had seen clients either in the university or in the Leicester Counselling Centre. I only had one private client (occasionally two) at any one time, and in the year in question I only had the one. I had to be sure that asking her and engaging her in the process would not cause any harm, and I needed to be as sure as I could be that she would stay in therapy with me long enough to conclude the process. I was fairly sure of my ground since the client was herself trained as a counsellor, and had made it clear that she saw our sessions going on for a while. I floated what I had in mind to her, and asked her to go away and consider the possibility rather than respond immediately. I made it clear that I would be no less a therapist for her if she decided against it. I left the issue for a few weeks to give her the chance to mull it over, trying to pick up in those intervening sessions any unconscious hint of the effect of my request upon her. She stayed with her initial decision and we began to record sessions, so that we both got used to the tape recorder before we settled on a session that I would transcribe for the six supervisors who had agreed to take part.

I am aware that my decision to undertake this will shock some readers, particularly those who believe that such a course of action distorts the transference, or even that there was no way of really knowing whether my client was agreeing just to please me. Certainly one of the supervisors slated me in his chapter, and implied that I was subjecting a client who had been sexually abused to further abuse. I once spoke about the project to a meeting of the graduates of a psychodynamic course in London, and received a very mixed reception. I remain convinced, as I hope to show here, that the process was in fact a very enriching one both for myself as a therapist and for the client, and therefore for our work together. It helped greatly in unlocking the process, in a way that my continuing to work without engaging in the project may or may not have done.

My client, to whom we decided together to give the name Ruth, requested a copy of each taped session. Following the practice of doing this that I had heard of from Windy Dryden, I was happy to do that. That in itself was helpful. Following one particular taped session, Ruth said that she had felt the session was very helpful and that it would be a good session to present for supervision. I had thought the same myself, although for different reasons. I set about transcribing it, in the course of which I realised to my horror just how much I had spoken in the session, and how it seemed to me that I had to some extent been floundering. Yet Ruth had thought it very helpful. This bore out some research that Moira Walker had done for her psychotherapy degree, which showed that there are times when therapists think they have had a good session but their client does not feel the same way, or vice versa.

Without revealing any of the session, I consulted an acquaintance in a different line of work from Ruth in order to build up a disguise for her since her work was part of the issue. I gave Ruth the transcript of the session together with a preamble sketching what a supervisor would need to know about the therapy previous to the session in question. I altered some of the preamble as a result of her suggestions, and removed one sentence from the actual session that might have given a clue to her identity to one other person. The material went to the six supervisors and we continued with the therapy while I waited for their questions. When these came they were of course just addressed to me, and need not to involve Ruth. One of the supervisors did not realise that the occupation we had chosen was a disguise, and because he was familiar with that occupation himself, he was concerned the details would reveal her identity. I knew then that our disguise was watertight.

One supervisor insisted we meet face-to-face and record our session, which seemed to me to give him an unfair advantage over the others, but I complied. He was the one person in the whole five books who was unable to write anything, because the recording did not work. It was a disappointment, but given the extra edge that meeting personally might have given him over the other five perhaps that was just as well in the end.

As the chapters from the five supervisors came to me, it was clear that since Ruth was already part of the process, the most obvious way of working on their comments was to share them with her. It would have been patently artificial to suddenly introduce an exercise (as two supervisors suggested) into a therapy that had up to then been simply conversational. Ruth and I needed to work on the exercises together, and to that end I gave her each contribution to read at fortnightly intervals. I started with the first I had received back, the stinging destruction of my part in the session by the communicative psychotherapist. I thought he went over the top in applying his theoretical stance. I had once taken part in a supervision session with Robert Langs (1993), the psychoanalyst who had developed the communicative approach, and what the supervisor said was par for the course. He told me I should stop seeing Ruth and refer her to someone else. This hurt and I was really hesitant about giving his piece to Ruth, or even using it at all. But the latter course of action would have been to invalidate the project, just because it was severe criticism of my work. A supervisor might have to act to prevent damage to a client. When Ruth came to the session after she had read that chapter, she was incensed. Not only did she disagree, she valued our work together and that session in particular. How could this supervisor think he knew better than she did what was right for her?

The other contributions were interesting. They extended our understanding, although in some ways the advice they gave was contradictory, such as the supervisor whose orientation was Kohut's psychoanalytic self-psychology (1971) and the person-centred supervisor. Each gave completely different advice about dealing with Ruth's request for a hug at the end of the session, where I was unsure how best to respond.

The cognitive-behavioural therapist suggested I set Ruth various homework tasks. I gave her a few weeks to work on these, but although they were of interest to her, she was generally sceptical of the emphasis on identifying and analysing negative thoughts. She wondered why there appeared to be no interest in her positive thoughts, which gave her a sense of her worth. The most significant contribution was from the family therapist, who suggested various tasks related to Ruth's family tree. Ruth gained considerable insight and relief from the genogram that she then compiled. It helped her to think not only how she had been affected by her upbringing, but also how much her parents would have been by theirs.

In both the series I have described, some books have been received better than others. The same is true of a third series I edited for Open University Press on the use of counselling skills for different professions, where initially I tried as far as possible to choose people who had not published before. Some produced very good texts; others found that writing was much more difficult than they had imagined, and fell away.

But if I have been fortunate in writing some books that have had wide appeal, my particular favourites are those that in terms of sales have actually been a flop! The irony is that they comprise my most original work, and are the books that I would have wished to be remembered by. They are, in my opinion, some of the best work I have written. The one closest to my heart, and the one that perhaps for me encapsulates my search for understanding in the broadest sense, is in its third incarnation. I conclude this chapter with the story of how it has come to be.

As a result of the editing work I had done for Darton, Longman and Todd on Frank Lake's *Tight Corners*, I had compiled a reader on pastoral care and counselling, consulting a number of pastoral counsellors and academics, asking them to select the three readings they would most like to see reproduced. It was fairly straightforward work and potentially a useful addition to the literature, selling its first print run but not reprinted. Lesley Riddle of DLT followed this up by asking if I could write a book on personal development for pastors.

I agreed, but once I started to write I found it impossible to stay with the agreed outline. I did not want to re-hash *The Presenting Past*, and I was more interested in James Fowler's *Stages of Faith* (1981). His research showed the parallels in terms of faith development with Erikson's stages of psychological development (stages that had influenced me, too, in the first edition of *The Presenting Past*) and with Kohlberg's stages of moral development (1981). Other stage theories like those of Freud, Jung and others suggested similar perspectives on personal development.

I chose therefore to write about the development of faith, drawing critically upon Fowler, and doing what I do best, making these ideas more accessible to a British readership. Foolishly I hoped that I was writing a book that would be relevant to the Church, but also to the counselling profession. It turned out to be neither! It had been a mistake to go for another clever scriptural title, *Towards the Fullness of Christ*. DLT must have ordered a rather hopeful print run because first year sales were reasonable, but then the book went into rapid decline. I received a letter from DLT to say they were going to pulp their remaining copies, but they could send them to me if I wished. I did so wish, and a number of huge boxes of the book duly arrived at my office, 1000 copies in all! I decided I would take them with me whenever I had speaking engagements, and offer them at a pound each to students at Vaughan College and to students on a ministry training course that I taught on every summer vacation. I sold every one of them and got more income that way than I did from the royalties when the book was in print!

Nevertheless, there was something about the book that had got hold of me. I knew it was not right as it was, and I had already come to question stage theory, as is obvious from the second edition of *The Presenting Past* (1998). Yet I thought the book contained the germ of something better, and that it was worth working on again. I began to see a wider application for the theories I had been discussing and a new way of working with them, which was much more original than anything I had yet written. I approached SPCK for whom I had not written for some years to suggest a revised edition of the book.

In 1992, I had the one and only sabbatical that Leicester University ever allowed me, and in that term I wrote much of the book *D.W. Winnicott* (1995b) for Sage, while *The Fullness of Christ* became a very different book, *Living Illusions: A Psychology of Belief* (1993a). I drew upon many different ideas, including the special subject that I had studied as part of my degree at Oxford – mysticism and the *via negativa*. The first print run sold out in its entirety, but not sufficiently quickly for SPCK to consider a second print run. A book about which I now felt more assured again hit the dust.

The second incarnation of the book was not specifically Christian, although SPCK is a Christian publishing house. But then neither was *Still Small Voice*. I tried hard to avoid alienating readers by any type of critical dogmatism about their Christian faith, and I spent a number of hours trying to get the tone of the very last paragraph of the book right. I wanted to leave completely open the question of the existence of God, in such a way that neither supported an atheistic stance nor a theistic one. I was trying to stay true to the 'unknowing' (which is more than 'not knowing') of the *via negativa* mystics. In the end I was satisfied, particularly with the very last sentence: 'Do the complexities of all these levels and experiences of belief make it too simple to say there may be nothing there?' (1993a: 187). Even then one review, despite it being generally favourable, particularly vexed me when it ended with the observation that it was a pity that I had not answered the final question at the end of the book!

Although the book went out of print, I taught day work-shops on its thesis and they seemed to go well. I wanted to ensure that it stayed in print, and I approached Colin Whurr, at the time one of the few remaining independent publishers in the field, to suggest a third edition. It would involve re-writing it yet again, because I was by now fine-tuning my ideas and I wanted to publish it outside the religious stable, hoping it would reach a different reader-ship. I will always be thankful that Colin agreed and that as a consequence the book remains available still through John Wiley, although at a price which I doubt many would be prepared to pay! The book as it stands now, *Illusion: A Psychodynamic Interpretation of Thinking and Belief* (2000a) is the one I would most want to be remembered by, although ironically it has sold almost the fewest copies of anything I have written. I still conduct day workshops on the themes of the book, using poetry, prose and music, which perhaps is one way I can still communicate what I believe to be really important ideas.

There have been other disappointments, but as any publisher knows, that is the name of the game. I got to a point when I was tired of writing and editing. 'No more,' I said, 'I have retired. There is too much on the market. I should bow out gracefully.' My late wife Moira used to tease me, saying I would never give up writing, but I was determined to do so, apart from new editions of existing books.

Until out of the blue a different publisher, with whom I had not previously worked, made contact and took me out to lunch. 'Have you got a book in you?' I was asked. 'I have not,' I replied, 'I'm not writing any more.' 'And in any case,' I said, 'I am now interested in the way psycho-analytic theory is applied to the study of film and litera-ture,' explaining that I was really enjoying teaching a WEA course on 'Shakespeare on the Couch'. Of course there was a book in that, and the publisher seized upon it, without even seeing what I had written as part of my lecture material. I did not see myself as a Shakespearean scholar, or as a psychoanalytic literary critic, but I wrote the book and it received a fair enough welcome in some circles. More importantly for me, it led to working (as a pensioner postgraduate student) on a PhD.

I tell these stories of some of the books that bear my name, not to promote them, but to show my attempts to make accessible to the counselling community ideas from psychoanalysis and elsewhere that have influenced my psychodynamic practice. I am aware that I was approached to write at a time when counselling was beginning to find its feet and flourish. I had the opportunity of writing some of the first British texts in the field of psychodynamic counselling, books that have been adopted as standard texts by a number of courses. It amazes me that they have remained in print, and have not yet been superseded by books that others have contributed to the field, which are just as good as if not better than mine. It appears that once a book becomes a standard text, it tends to stay in that position. I have been in the right place at the right time.

7

A finger in different pies

I left BAC completely in 1982, for reasons explained in Chapter 4 and because I was stretched in several directions by the increasing demands on the counselling service, as well as by the need to strengthen and expand the counselling training at the university's two adult education centres. I began to think about a change of direction. I wanted to write more and to shed some of my clinical work in favour of teaching. I had been ten years in the post, become more settled in myself and was aware that a mixed economy – some clinical work, some writing and some teaching – suited me better than seeing twenty or so clients each week. Indeed, I have often said since to supervisees who are experiencing the first signs of burn-out that to be involved in at least one other type of work, related or otherwise, might begin to lessen the pressure.

It may seem odd to those working in the huge universities we have today but Leicester, like many other universities even in the early 1980s, was still relatively small in numbers and senior figures were much more accessible. Since the beginning I had been responsible not to the health service, except for day-to-day matters, but to the vice-chancellor. At that time it was Maurice Shock, with whom

I got on quite well. So I went to see him. He had already been responsive in allowing me the time away from the university on BAC business, which probably averaged half a day a week. I had some confidence that if I explained to him that I was actually doing two jobs and that one of them had to go that I would be taken seriously. That was indeed the case: he replied that I needed to move on at this stage in my career, and that the obvious move was to transfer to adult education so that I could develop and manage the counselling programme.

His support helped, but it was not sufficient. I was up against tight budgeting despite the fact that my courses were already bringing in considerable income. Since I was arranging the programme, I had been setting the fees slightly higher than the fees for other subjects in the department, in order to cover all the hourly costs of my own teaching and that of the growing number of sessional tutors. In addition, while the head of the adult education department was very affable and thought it a good idea to take me on, he was rather laid back and very slow to make it happen. The Warden of Vaughan College, who had invited me to teach in the first instance, was a senior member of the department, and he began to apply pressure from within. But the move would never have taken place had it not been for a discussion with Simon Phipps, now Bishop of Lincoln.

When I was at Sussex University, Simon was Bishop of Horsham and he had taken a particular interest in the university, mainly because of his interest in international development. Although that was not my area, we had seen each other in the university several times, and began to meet socially as my wife Valerie and I were invited to dinner. I had moved to Leicester before he moved to Lincoln, but we stayed in touch, and when he was 'translated' (as they say in the Church) to his new diocese we were invited to dinner again. Simon had in the intervening years married Mary Welch, a Jungian analyst of some repute, whom we had met on one occasion at his home in Sussex.

To Mary his move had seemed as if to a therapeutic wilderness and she was equally keen to meet up with another therapist.

Simon wished to develop pastoral care and counselling in his diocese, and we talked about how this might be done. He met regularly with three other East Midland diocesan bishops and he proposed to them the appointment of a director of pastoral care and counselling for all four dioceses, with myself in mind for the post. A full-time post was out of the question, since the Church was as strapped for funds as the university, but if the four dioceses could afford to pay for two days of my university salary, I could work from the adult education department to develop a network of training and resources for pastoral care and pastoral counselling in the region.

All four bishops agreed to his plan in outline, and each one in turn asked to meet me. I was already known to the Bishop of Leicester who had succeeded Ronald Williams, and he had been much more understanding about the work I was doing. He had restored some of my trust in the Church. Simon Phipps met with the vice-chancellor and the head of adult education, and everything seemed to fit. But before a final decision was made, teams from all four dioceses attended a two-day conference in Derbyshire that I facilitated. I used a large-scale simulation exercise to look at the different pressures on clergy and diocesan staffs. As a result, three of the diocesan teams returned to their respective bishops agreeing to the proposal, but the team from Leicester diocese reacted differently. Leicester opted out of the scheme, leaving it in the balance whether the other three dioceses would continue to fund it. They did, enabling me to transfer on a temporary contract to adult education, a temporary contract that was renewed for twelve years until it was made permanent.

In my new post I was to spend two days a week advancing pastoral counselling and training for pastoral counselling mainly for the clergy in the three dioceses, although lay men and women were involved in both sets of developments. A link person was appointed in each diocese (two in Lincolnshire) so that we might work as a team, meeting regularly to share thinking and practice. This involved considerable travel on my part, since I started to teach short courses for clergy and lay people myself in the East Midlands through six-week courses, adapting the training with which I was already familiar.

So, after twelve years I was back working in the Church, although largely with an administrative and teaching function. I was licensed by Simon Phipps, restoring the position that had been denied me by my own diocesan bishop. The post led to other developments. I began to teach on a summer school for training for ministry (where I once more resumed a liturgical role); I published a book on clergy appraisal (1989); and I worked with a number of senior diocesan staff both in the area and further afield to develop their skills in annual reviews of their clergy: appraisal was the flavour of the year, introduced also into the university although in a rather amateur way. Our East Midlands team initiated an annual meeting of advisers in pastoral care and counselling throughout the country at Launde Abbey in Leicestershire, that I believe continued for several years. In 1986, I moved out to East Leicestershire and agreed to help out in the village churches in the area. This led to a new niche for myself in ministry, where I was able to handle in a way I could not conceive possible when I was younger the mismatch between my own very radical beliefs and the conventions of a parish church.

It was not that I returned, as some might say, 'to the faith'. I thought then, as much as I had done earlier, that what had once been for me '*the* truth' no longer mattered to me as to whether or not it was actually true. What was important to me was that religious beliefs had the status of myths in the sense that they were attempts to find what was true, and that the different stories and doctrines could be interpreted in different ways in different situations and at different points in life. But then psychoanalysis is also a myth: it may or may not be true in its particulars, but it points to possibilities, and if it is to be of any value we need to find for ourselves what seems true. This too may change in different situations and at different times. All this was to be expressed much more clearly in the way I worked over the years in my book *Illusion* (2000a).

For myself, I valued music and literature just as much, religious or not, as conveying for many people a sense of some truth (whatever that is). One day in 1989 Moira Walker suggested that it would be lovely just to have a weekend away, reading and relaxing, a sort of retreat like religious people do (she was much more sceptical than me about religion) where she could recharge her batteries. I replied that of course we could run such a retreat for those in the caring professions, albeit a secular one, drawing upon literature and music.

As we talked, we could see that it could be structured like a religious retreat, such as I had attended when preparing for ordination. Instead of spiritual talks from a conductor, we would include three half-hour sessions of words and music on a particular theme. There would be plenty of free space where people could either be quiet on their own in silence, or if they wished mix with the other retreatants. We would have a couple of sessions providing opportunities for meditation and guided fantasy for those who wished to attend, a walk in the Leicestershire countryside, a late-night story each evening by candlelight, and a 'let your hair down' game on one evening before the story. Just as retreat conductors offered times for spiritual guidance, we would offer an hour to each person over the course of the weekend, if they wanted to use the opportunity: fifteen minutes the first evening, half an hour on the full day, and a further fifteen minutes on the last morning.

There was a retreat house near where I lived, Launde Abbey, and I had known the warden since he attended my first small group on Freud, which I had taught when I first moved to Leicester. He welcomed the idea, and allocated a separate building for us, allowing our people to engage in the more religious activities of the main house if they chose to, but they would not have religion forced upon them.

Instead of recharging batteries for Moira it was, of course, for us yet another commitment, but a very rewarding one all the same. Our first weekend was called 'A country retreat' and we filled all twelve places. Others followed on the theme of winter, the sea, and isles and islands.

These retreats proved popular and we conducted two retreats a year at Launde. For some people they were deep experiences, and we learned how to use the offer of an hour's individual 'counselling' to help those who took advantage of it to work on a particular current issue. We were usually able to identify an area to think about in the initial fifteen-minute meeting, which could be reflected upon over the weekend; we encouraged talking about it more deeply in the half-hour session the next day; and we pulled the threads together in the fifteen-minute session on the last morning. This proved a remarkably effective way of working, helped of course by the fact that many of those who attended were counsellors themselves.

I believe this sense of being able to integrate my former career as a priest, at least in some respects, with my career as a therapist might well have continued had it not been for yet another series of knock-downs from the Church. The close working relationship that Moira and I had contrasted with my relationship with Valerie my wife, who had married me as a future priest and never really understood my role as a counsellor and therapist. Others have found the same I think, that the counselling/therapy world tends to be a somewhat inaccessible place to those not in it, not helped by issues about confidentiality and the intensity of some therapeutic relationships. Moira had become for me not just a colleague, but also a companion. I had to take the most difficult decision of my life: whether to hurt and undermine my wife by separating, or stay in a relationship which, although it had worked well enough for home-making and raising a family who had now become independent, failed to meet my intellectual needs. I regretted deeply what I had to do, but knew that I had to do it; otherwise, I would have been in a marriage that would never give me what I had found with Moira. It was a major step, but one that developed me as a writer, teacher and therapist.

In late 1989, I moved into a flat where I lived on my own for twelve months. It was in a near-total Muslim area, one of the most friendly and open communities I have ever lived in. After a year I moved into Moira's house, with the intention of seeking a divorce and us marrying. It was then, out of the blue, that I received in my office a letter from the new Bishop of Lincoln, appointed after Simon Phipps had retired. Since I was now living with Moira he said he had no choice but to remove my licence. The letter was not marked 'private and confidential', and might have been opened by my secretary. Soon after that I was at a meeting of the council of the East Midlands ministry training course, and the chair, the Archdeacon of Leicester, referred publicly, without any pretext, to the 'fact' that I had celebrated communion at Launde when I no longer had a licence. I would therefore not be allowed to use Launde Abbey any more for our retreats. What he said was completely untrue, since I had not conducted any kind of service since my separation, and never at Launde. And why say this at a meeting where it was irrelevant? I was so incensed at having been maligned in public that I resigned from the council (which is perhaps what the chair wanted), and began to wind down my role with the East Midland dioceses. In any case, my work in the university had begun to encroach on the days the churches paid for, so it was only fair to do so.

In 1997 we were allowed to return to holding retreats at Launde, perhaps because we had been married several years! We conducted several more before we moved to Dorset in July 2000.

I remained outside BAC for ten years but re-joined in 1995 when my former teaching colleague Alan Lilley, then vice-chair of BAC, told me that there was to be a new category of Fellow of the association, and that I would be nominated as long as I was a member. This was an honour I could not refuse, presumably for my contribution to counselling through my books rather than anything else. In due course at the AGM in 1995 I joined others such as Audrey Newsome, Brian Thorne and Bernard Ratigan in receiving the first awards.

I may have been back in the fold, but I remained critical of some aspects of the association. I have explained in Chapter 4 how the Leicester courses could not qualify for accreditation, and I was becoming increasingly concerned at the stranglehold that I believed BAC was having on the development of counselling in terms of its regulations for accreditation. The accreditation scheme that BAC had introduced in 1988 failed to recognise that universities have their own procedures and high standards for approving and monitoring courses. I knew from contact with other university course directors that a number of them were concerned that BAC would not accept their university status as evidence of sufficient quality for accreditation. For example, I was the external examiner for the University of Cambridge course, which like mine only had one permanent staff member, Tony Storey; and I gathered Ellen Noonan at Birkbeck College, University of London, thought the same.

Tony Storey and I organised a conference at Madingley Hall, Cambridge, to which we invited a number of leaders of university counselling courses. That meeting and a second the following year were well attended and proved productive in sharing ideas, including for the most part agreement with what Tony and I thought. However, there was no stopping BAC's march towards standardisation, and in time we all had to submit, since the market place dictated that if we could not offer an accredited course, students would go elsewhere. As I have explained earlier Leicester continued with its open policy; the majority of students still attended courses that were not accredited, but there was an accredited diploma for those who wanted to apply.

One particular outcome to our meetings was significant. At the second conference, I had a request from Professor Digby Tantam, chair of the new Universities Psychotherapy Association (UPA), asking if he could attend. Digby had not realised that there were flourishing counselling programmes in universities as well as the psychotherapy courses that had founded UPA. I think it was the Cambridge meeting that prompted the widening of the association to become the Universities Psychotherapy and Counselling Association (UPCA). It was some years before BAC took the decision to include psychotherapy in its title, which came about through a proposal I was delighted to be able to second and speak to at the AGM in Cardiff in 2000. I am glad to have played a small part in bringing psychotherapy and counselling under the same two umbrellas. Since UPCA was a section of the UK Council for Psychotherapy, counselling had some recognition there too.

Although I lost contact with the Rugby psychotherapy conferences after the first symposium in 1982, I was brought back into contact with the developing Standing Conference in 1991. Moira Walker and I were promoting a psychotherapy qualification at the University of Leicester. In order to achieve recognition for our graduands, we needed the training to be accepted into membership of one of the sections of the UK Standing Conference.

Despite having a psychodynamic core to our syllabus, we were not confident that our requirements for students to undertake once-weekly personal therapy would be acceptable to the then psychoanalytic and psychodynamic psychotherapy (PPP) section, where twice-weekly sessions were the norm. We therefore approached the humanistic and integrative section (then known as HIPS), knowing that the Bath Centre for Psychotherapy and Counselling, which we had consulted in setting up our course, was a member. Moira went to her first meeting of HIPS, and was discouraged by the chair saying that we should not lay claim to the title 'psychodynamic', since some of their trainings were also psychodynamic.

I did not understand what he was getting at, but his manner had put Moira off, so with some hesitation we approached the PPP section. Applicants were encouraged to attend their meetings as observers, but were not allowed to speak. At one meeting there was discussion about the merits of once-weekly or twice-weekly therapy (that is, for clients), and someone observed that outside London twice-weekly therapy was rare. A rather large, elegantly dressed, white-haired *grande dame* from one of the London psychoanalytic centres said in a loud voice, 'Well, we all know that people living in the provinces are a special case.' I could not keep silent. I burst out, 'Well, some of us in the provinces think that London is a special case!' But it seemed to do no harm, and we were eventually accepted into membership.

Although we were very new members and had no part to play in the decision, we were represented at the extraordinary general meeting when the Standing Conference became the UK Council for Psychotherapy in 1993. When we joined the PPP section, membership included the British Institute for Psychoanalysis and other psychoanalytic trainings in London such as the then Lincoln Centre, the British Association of Psychotherapists and the Tavistock Clinic, as well as a large number of psychoanalytic psychotherapy courses such as the Westminster Pastoral Foundation or the then London Centre for Psychotherapy, and ourselves – we preferred to style our course psychodynamic rather than psychoanalytic. It became clear to me that certain psychoanalytic societies and institutes saw themselves as in a different league, not so much to other members of the section (although there was something of that) but to the members of the other sections of the Standing Conference, such as the humanistic and integrative section and the behavioural section. In 1992, certain members such as the Institute of Psychoanalysis and the Tavistock decided to break away to form what is now known as the British Psychoanalytic Council, and to have its own register of qualified members.

As I saw it at the time, Michael Pokorny of the London Centre for Psychotherapy and chair of the Standing Conference, together with other members of the PPP section that still remained in the Conference, saw the breakaway movement as an attempt to vaunt their status over other psychoanalytic and psychodynamic organisations. As I listened to the debate, it seemed to me that what I was witnessing was a turf war amongst the different London psychoanalytic and psychodynamic groups. Be that as it may, clearly other sections thought the same as ours and so the UK Council for Psychotherapy was created with its own (rival?) register.

One consequence of the formation of UKCP was that we and our graduates were grandparented on to this new register as psychodynamic psychotherapists. I had over ten years earlier sought membership of the Guild of Psychotherapists through the training and supervision I had already received. The sticking point had been that my regular supervision with a member of the Institute of Psychoanalysis was not deemed sufficient: it had to be with one of their own supervisors, none of whom lived near Leicester. I have no patience with these distinctions as long as supervision is good, and I did not pursue my application. Now for the first time I had a kind of title, in addition to being a fellow of BAC, and I had some legitimacy. Yes, even I was seduced at that time by status.

Actually, I am not someone who gets vexed about the line that demarcates counselling and psychotherapy, as my support for extending the titles of BAC(P) and UP(C)A shows. Nor am I now bothered how I should describe myself. It all smacks too much for me of the Church. I chaired a working party for BACP in 2001 on the distinction between psychotherapy and counselling. As a group we were unanimous that the wrong way of approaching the question was to try and identify what is distinctive about counselling and about psychotherapy. Both activities are so similar that the more relevant distinction we made was between more experienced and less experienced counsellors and psychotherapists. Rather than a specific training alone, it is experience, personal development and growing knowledge that marks the more mature counsellor/therapist from the trainee and the newly qualified. I wrote up our conclusions for what was then the *Counselling and Psychotherapy Journal* (2001: 16–17). Despite that working party, from time to time this debate still goes on within BACP, showing no knowledge of our report. I reproduced our main findings in my book *Our Desire of Unrest* (2009b: 164–5).

I have taken a number of roles from time to time over the last twenty-five years within BACP, UKCP and UPCA, including chairing for a short while the research committee of BACP (not really my métier), vice-chair of UPCA and membership of UKCP's editorial board, mainly sifting through proposals for publications in the series UKCP publishes with Karnac. I have respect for all these organisations, each of which has different strengths and weaknesses.

One of the particular strengths of BACP is its ethical framework and its complaints procedure. I was involved in the latter from some point in the 1990s to 2015. The first occasion was when Alan Jamieson, deputy chief executive of BAC, asked me if I would sit on an adjudication panel to hear a complaint. I had up to that time had no experience of any type of adjudication. I had no legal knowledge and I had no training. I agreed because I was told I would simply be a panel member. As I recall there was little paperwork beforehand, and when I arrived at BAC I met Alan as clerk to the hearing and the other two panel members. It was at that point that Alan asked me if I would chair the panel! I protested that I didn't know what to do and it would be better if one of the others did so. But they did not wish to either. Never one to shirk a challenge I accepted the brief, and we proceeded to the adjudication with a sketchy agenda in front of me. The hearing involved having to make a decision at one point about whether or not to accept late evidence. There was no procedure to follow as there is now in such an event, but we decided to accept the evidence. Indeed, it proved crucial in making our decision in favour of the complainant.

I imagined that this had been a one-off request, but a little later (I wish I could remember the year) I was contacted out of the blue by the newly appointed officer overseeing complaints, Gráinne Griffin. She had heard that I had chaired a hearing already and she asked me to chair an adjudication that was to take place on the south coast. Once again I agreed. This time the proceedings were recorded on tape, and there was a much clearer process. I was then asked time and again and became one of a number of senior members chairing adjudications and pre-hearing assessment panels. We began to undergo training of a similar nature to that required of local magistrates. Gráinne built up a complaints department that became a model for other organisations. With increasing litigation and the possibility of judicial review, various procedures were made more watertight.

I regretted it deeply when Gráinne suddenly and mysteriously left BACP, since as the clerk to many of the adjudications I chaired she showed wisdom, appropriate humour and a gentle Irish touch. It was a pleasure working for many years with her and her principal assistant Fay.

One result of her sudden departure was the end to what had seemed to me a promising development, a mediation process with trained mediators to handle some of the complaints that BACP receives. There had been some experiments in this direction, since both Moira Walker and myself had conducted a type of mediation at one point, although we were again not trained for the task.

As the complaints culture became more widespread, BACP had to handle situations ranging from inadvertent and unthinking mistakes to the serious abuse of clients. Since I also chaired pre-hearing panels where decisions had to be made whether or not to accept complaints, I came across a number of situations where mediation would have been much the better way of handling what seemed to me a relatively minor infringement of the ethical code. Sometimes the opportunity for a client to voice his or her complaint to the therapist, and receive a sincere apology on the part of the therapist, would be sufficient for learning on the part of the counsellor, and for a sense of justice on the part of the client. For minor infringements that technically breach the ethical framework, it would be much less anxiety provoking for client and member, and considerably less expensive of time, staff and money. Like other panel members I have sometimes thought, 'There but for the grace of God, go I', when unthinking mistakes have led to a formal and weighty procedure that assumes for both parties the significance of a lawsuit.

When I first chaired adjudications, there were several codes of ethics to cover counselling, supervision, training and organisations. It seemed to me that at times such codes gave rise to a sort of legalism: what precisely did the wording of a clause mean? I know of course that that is the way the law works. Perhaps that is inevitable as soon as lawyers are involved, but I thought the new Ethical Framework in 2010 was a vast improvement, placing as much emphasis on principles as on specific infringements. However, my experience has been that since its introduction, the old legalism has crept back in, since every finding has to be linked specifically to one or more of the clauses, making the Ethical Framework again more legalistic. I realise that issues of due process and justice make this inevitable, but it does not sit well with the principles in therapeutic practice of acceptance and being non-judgemental. I have been at BACP meetings where person-centred representatives have declared as much, and I have come to think that they have a point. In their prescient article in 2000, Dryden et al. were concerned that the then BACP code of ethics was becoming 'ever more detailed and prescriptive' (2000: 474). It is difficult to avoid the same conclusion when it comes to the handling of some breaches of the present ethical code. For various reasons in late 2015, after over twenty years, I resigned from my involvement with complaints procedures.

I have in this chapter strayed into the present century, when I had retired from the University of Leicester. To complete the story of my time in Leicester, during the 1990s I was at last given a permanent contract in adult education, and after twenty-five years working for the university promoted to senior lecturer. When I was joined in the department by Moira Walker, we had invaluable help from two administrators, whose eye for detail meant that they freed us up as the bureaucratic demands increased. Many changes were taking place as the department lost its independence and became part of the School of Education. Our head of department took redundancy and the shrinking academic staff (some had been moved to other departments) chose his successor. But when that person needed to quit and a new head was as it seemed to me foisted on us, my patience snapped. After all, I felt that my programme had contributed to the department and to the university, and I thought that we as the staff of the department were being sidelined. After an admittedly rather bad-tempered and perhaps inappropriate email from me to the new departmental head (it is the problem with emails), and an equally stinging response to me from one of the deputy vice-chancellors, it is little wonder that on the same evening as reading his response I found myself experiencing the strangest sensations I had ever had. It was as if I was drunk, although I had had only one glass of wine. When Moira returned from an evening out with a colleague she knew something was radically wrong and whisked me off to the emergency doctor. Before the evening was out I found myself in the admission ward of Leicester General Hospital. My time at Leicester was coming to an end.

8

Working towards an ending

'Minor stroke, major warning,' said the senior houseman as he examined me. I felt relatively okay, if shaken, but in the night a more severe attack left me paralysed down my left side. Fortunately, it lasted under twenty-four hours, and, as suddenly as it had ceased to function, my right hand was again able to grip a glass of water.

We had always planned that I would retire when I was sixty-two or sixty-three, which was still three years away. Knowing the importance of planning endings in therapy, I had already been letting go of most of my teaching responsibilities as I prepared the ground for retirement, and for someone else to take over. I obviously could not return to work straightaway, and when the new academic year started Moira Walker had to take over my role, while another stepped in to cover my supervision on the psychotherapy course. Only my optional module had to be cancelled. However, I continued to see my clients one morning a week at the Leicester Counselling Centre. The university offered me early retirement on a full pension. I do not know whether this was because they were worried that I had been over-taxed running such a large programme, then asking for more support but not getting it, or whether they were glad to see the back of me, since I had become a thorn in their flesh or even a pain in the arse.

Moira did not want to continue on her own in the department, which was in any case in the process of being slimmed down with no clear idea of what would happen to the counselling programme. She then had had to take on a heavy load. When the opportunity arose, she applied for and was offered the post that Ellen Noonan had relinquished on retiring from Birkbeck College, London. The post was never as happy as Leicester had been since many of the sessional tutors were still attached to Ellen and I gather did not make Moira feel very welcome. But her move made it possible for us to relocate earlier than we had planned to Dorset, where Moira had been brought up and where I had my first memories, having been evacuated to Shaftesbury in 1944.

We continued to run our residential supervision course, both in Leicestershire and in Dorset, where we had prepared the ground for our move by liaising with the Dorset counselling and psychotherapy association. I was free now to work much of the time on editing the *Core Concepts* series, and we each started a small independent practice of therapy and supervision.

Within a year I started teaching for the Workers Educational Association: short courses in which I was able to adapt courses I had taught at Leicester to what was largely a 'lay' audience. But within two years the WEA had decided that, since I had no formal qualifications as a counselling teacher, they could no longer employ me! Undaunted I decided to set up my own course with the same group and we continued to meet January and February for eight weeks for 'Film on the couch', a course where we watched films and discussed them from a psychoanalytic point of view with myself supplying digests of psychoanalytic ideas and interpretations. Although only a few of those who attended were therapists, we could of course all draw upon our life experiences and we had some very good discussions. I taught the course using different films for ten years before deciding to call it a day.

I began to teach on an integrative psychotherapy course at Bournemouth University. The course closed after one cohort, which I think was right, since I was (and am) concerned about Masters' degrees where students' experience as counsellors is rather limited. A number of us tried to float a counselling degree in cooperation with a college of further education, but this was axed just as we had completed all the necessary documentation. It was an early sign of what was happening and going to happen in other universities. However, a few years later I was appointed visiting professor and engaged to teach the talking therapies on an introductory Masters course on clinical psychology. Covering the subject in four hours is some task!

Having been active participants in the work of the Leicester Counselling Centre, we were keen to use that experience and accept an invitation to become trustees of a low-cost service that a colleague was starting in Dorchester. In addition, Moira led a major project in Poole for survivors of abuse, where I have been a supervisor and am now a patron. I return to the importance of these services later in this chapter.

In semi-retirement I was able to exercise some control over how much I did, no longer carried along by the demands of the university. I was involved also in local community activities that were totally different from counselling and therapy, although my teaching experience helped in one organisation far removed from the consulting room where I became the training officer for the local Coastwatch. I still undertook adjudications and assessments for BACP, and I conducted day workshops in different parts of the country on an occasional basis. It was a good way to work towards complete retirement from counselling and therapy, when that day finally comes.

I have had my share of physical ill health but have remained generally fit, enjoying holidays abroad, making new friends, being part of a relatively small community living in a house with a wonderful view over the sea. All seemed fair set, but in late 2009 Moira was diagnosed with a life-threatening lymphoma. For the next year she underwent punishing treatment, spending four weeks at one point in complete isolation, although I spent most of each day with her, trying to encourage her towards recovery. She seemed to come through it and be clear of the cancer, but the possibility of its return hung over us with a checkup every six months. Each one brought temporary relief, until in November 2013 she was told that the lymphoma had returned. She had some dedicated doctors who battled against the cancer and she again was put through the mill, in some ways much more severely than previously, spending more time than before in hospital. While I was able to continue with my private work, my clients and supervisees had to put up moveable appointments, and I only lost one for whom my situation (which was obviously worrying despite my attempts not to involve my clients) was too reminiscent of his own experience.

In March 2013, Moira rapidly declined and our immensely rich and productive relationship came to an end. Her funeral was attended by many friends and colleagues, and I did not hold back my grief at losing a friend, companion and colleague of twenty-five years. But it was tempered in the weeks that followed by deep appreciation of the relationship we had had. If it surprised some people when I began a new relationship with another therapist who is now my wife, it was because having had so many fulfilling years, I believed that it would also be possible in a new relationship: one that was not the same and involved sharing in different interests that I had not had the same opportunity to share in before.

When Moira died, I was in the first year of researching a PhD on psychoanalytic interpretations of *A Midsummer Night's Dream*. I took a year out, but returned to this major project for the next three years. My two supervisors both taught English literature, so we together engaged in a fascinating dialogue between the two disciplines. Writing a PhD was very different from anything I had done before, however experienced I was as an author. I cannot count the number of drafts I submitted, but it was worthwhile and improved my thesis no end. The thesis was the icing on the cake of my principal interests that lie now in the relationship of psychoanalysis (itself in no way a monolithic discourse) with the arts.

Moira's death, unexpected given I was the older of the two of us and we always thought it would be me who would die first, brought home to me the uncertainties of life, and the unpredictability of my later years in terms of health. I still had a few clients in therapy, and was determined to see them through to a natural ending, but it seemed right not to land future clients with having to cope with their therapist's illness or death. I had already at one point spent five weeks in hospital with an apparently infected pacemaker, and that had not been easy for my clients. I therefore ended with the last client at her chosen time in December 2015. It was, however, strange having to turn down those who approached me for therapy. I continued offering supervision, and curiously my supervision practice expanded to fill the time vacated by the client hours. While I had always had reservations about a supervisor not being in practice, it appears that even without a formal qualification and accreditation some people still believe I might be a safe pair of hands.

When I taught from Erikson's 'ages of man', I used to take a session on the eighth final age, where the strengths he identifies are wisdom and renunciation. It must be for others to reckon whether or not I have any wisdom, but what I am particularly aware of is renunciation, gradually closing down as a teacher, therapist and supervisor, while at the same time enjoying the richness of so much else I want to read, hear and experience, as long as I have the energy and faculties to do so. As Erikson describes,

I find myself looking back over a working life in a field in which I have had opportunities that many of those who train today will never have.

Like many of my generation, I have lived through some of the best of times. Free education, advances in medicine, worldwide travel, technological and electronic miracles, and in my career the rapid expansion of counselling in this country. But I detect the signs that much of this is changing, and changing for the worse. If it is perhaps permissible to be a grumpy older man I conclude on a sober note. I have sometimes joked that old therapists do not die – they simply lose their patience. I do not believe that I have ever lost my patience with my patients/clients, but the reader will already have noted the occasions when in other settings I have lost it, sometimes with authorities, sometimes with organisations.

I have seen how courses in counselling, which at one time flourished in universities, have gone into decline, even closed; not necessarily because of low recruitment, but because universities no longer want them. I have watched over the years since I retired as my own University of Leicester first of all spent a long time appointing my replacement, and then concentrated more upon those counselling courses that lead to accreditation, with far less attention on the non-graduate courses that at their peak engaged the interest of so many who did not necessarily want to become professional counsellors and therapists. The basic non-graduate certificate had continued to enrol well, but in 2002 was closed down. The modular diploma lasted a little longer. The psychotherapy course went. In 2013, the university closed Vaughan College, where I spent so many happy years, and its operation in Northampton. In 2016, it engaged on a consultation process which itself felt like a sop to likely critics before deciding to axe many of the counselling courses, which I gather has outraged many current and ex-students. Various certificates in counselling developed since my time were due to finish by 2019.

Training for counselling is increasingly in the hands of the private sector. My fear for universities all those years ago has been borne out. Some of these training organisations are charities, and have to cover costs, even if they are not in the business of making profits. Nevertheless, the fees now charged for training are much larger than anything we had to ask for in the Leicester programme and I am sure are putting off those who can see that there are not enough salaried posts in the public sector. If low-cost courses affect the number of students able to undertake placements in counselling centres such as I have been associated with (many of whom stay on after graduation), then low-cost counselling will largely cease. Yet private practice is mushrooming. Look at the networking groups advertised by BACP. Many of them are for private practice.

It has been a privilege to have been involved in the development of three counselling services offering low-cost counselling. I admire greatly the work, dedication and skill of volunteer counsellors, many of them trainees, who often work with presentations that would at one time only have been considered suitable for experienced psychotherapists. Unpaid counsellors offer so much to a hard-pressed NHS and its rather poor mental health services where time and again I hear many reports of 'Steps 2 Wellbeing' as insufficient. I wonder how it can be that nobody in government has seen the possibilities that a relatively small outlay for salaries for a clinical director and an administrator, as well as premises, could offer a large number of trained and training counsellors, unable to find work but willing to give three or four hours a week to the relief of emotional suffering. I also wonder why BACP has not done more to draw attention to the resources that could be drawn upon to set up low-cost counselling centres. But perhaps I know the answer, because it was not really on the agenda even back in 1978 when I floated the idea to the then management committee. It has been career opportunities and the promotion of professional interests that has dominated BACP's agenda.

At the same time I appreciate much that BACP, UPCA and UKCP have achieved, and there is no doubt more that goes on now behind the scenes than I am aware of. Of the two major therapy associations, BACP and UKCP, I think BACP, despite the reservations I shall shortly outline, has the edge, partly because it is based not upon factional interests as have at some points dogged UKCP. It has led the way in integrating the different modalities working in different settings. Yet the way UKCP was founded on the basis of training institutes and organisations with their separate membership of their own graduates has the advantage that practitioners are better known personally to their peers, who can monitor their progress and the quality of their work in person rather than through fairly anonymous procedures as in BACP.

The weakness of BACP seems to me its increasing bureaucratisation. For example, its requirements for supervision of accredited members are laid down with little sense of the differences in practice and the experience of its members. Essential though supervision is in training and while gaining experience, I do not agree with the blanket requirements for supervision in BACP and I note the difference between them and UPCA, UKCP and the National Society for Counselling, all of which accept that supervision should be commensurate with the number of client hours, and according to the experience of the counsellor or therapist. Why is it necessary to have ninety minutes' supervision a month for a therapist like myself who after thirty to forty years' experience was only seeing two or three clients a week? An experienced counsellor or therapist, if a difficult or puzzling situation arises with a particular client, should know who to approach and when. At times I have had to provide supervision for ninety minutes a month for a practitioner who only has one client, just so that person can remain accredited. It seems to me that such rigid requirements are there to enable bureaucracy to run more smoothly and to turn the requirements for accreditation and registration into a tick-box exercise.

My second example is highlighted as I write, in a letter in *Therapy Today* from a former assessor of courses, individual counsellors and supervisors, resigning from the association. He notes that over thirty years he has 'witnessed a reduction in the requirements for accreditation and re-accreditation' (Murray, 2017: 17). He records how applicants for accreditation as supervisors once had to conduct a live supervision before a panel. I am reminded of requiring four tapes of supervision sessions when I taught the subject.

This correspondent also comments on the process for registration, and I have supervisees who have also complained at how easy it has become to tick boxes to re-register. Here my own interest is more personal. When I re-joined BAC in 1993, I was an individual member. Some time later I was demoted, I know not why, to associate member, but I was not unduly concerned. What's in a name? I was still a member. More recently, I was invited to become an individual member again in order to take the certificate of proficiency for entry on BACP's 'voluntary' register. In my application to be grandparented to individual member status I had submitted as requested a long letter setting out my training, my experience, my lengthy CV and my membership of other professional bodies where, for example, I had been registered by UKCP, and accredited by UPCA. I had ended my membership of those two bodies as I wound down my practice, since so many professional fees were involved, and I had decided to throw in my lot with BACP, to which I had devoted so much time and energy over the years.

For months I had no reply to that application and I eventually wrote to the then chair of BACP, thinking that as a Fellow I might have my concern noticed. I received instead a letter from someone in the appropriate department because the letter had been forwarded to him. The chair did not have the courtesy to reply.

I was then told that there was a new procedure, which rendered my long application superfluous. Instead, I had to tick a number of boxes on a short form indicating that

I accepted the Ethical Framework, etc., and then I would be made an individual member! I imagine it was too arduous bureaucratically to work through proper applications such as I and no doubt others had submitted. Anyone can tick the boxes, much as years before Bernard Manning had been accepted as a member. But my individual membership was not sufficient to stay in BACP while still in practice. As someone who had not undertaken a BACP accredited course, indeed as someone who had no formal qualifications whatsoever, I was required to take the certificate of proficiency within two years.

I have already explained my criticism of that certificate (see Chapter 4). Over and above it being yet another tick-box exercise that virtually anyone off the street can be prepared for through one or two tutorials or through reading a book, I felt it as an insult to have to take a test as a Fellow of BACP, as someone who had written the very books that some graduating from accredited courses had used, and as one who had been registered by UKCP and accredited by UPCA, and is currently registered as a Fellow of the National Counselling Society, in order to be registered through BACP. But if I did not take the test, I could not be registered and I could no longer be a member of BACP. Some voluntary register!

Of course, this does not just apply to myself. I know of one person who trained as a psychotherapist in an organisation that ran a parallel course for counsellors. The counselling course was accredited, but the psychotherapy course (leading to UKCP membership) was not. Yet the more highly trained psychotherapist in the same organisation (and no doubt her peers) was still required to take the certificate in order to join BACP.

I was not going to be forced into a position where I had to take a test, which I already regarded as a mistaken way of assessing applicants for registration. I knew of a number of other experienced counsellors who had also declined to take the test and left BACP. I joined the National Counselling

Society (NCS), which registered me as a Fellow on the strength of my CV, and I imagine because my work was known. I approached BACP again and this time a very courteous senior staff member tried to persuade me to take the certificate. My NCS registration was not recognised either, despite BACP's apparent wish to liaise with other similar organisations. A senior member of BACP wrote trying to persuade me, advancing the argument that eminence was no guarantee of safety or quality. He too had had the same reservations as I [had] but took the test in the end, as some senior members have. Much as I appreciated his attempts to argue the case, I replied that in my experience of the complaints process, accreditation was no guarantee of quality and safety, and I wondered how long it had been after the institution of the register that a registered member had had a complaint made against him or her. I also object strongly to being assessed by a computer. Where has the personal relationship gone in assessing the quality of a person's work? This is the worst type of manualised counselling, such as John Rowan and I had criticised in our book. It is the worst type of institutionalisation that Dryden et al. had predicted would be the future for BACP in their article in 2000.

I was admitted as an individual member in June 2015, and allowed two years to take the test. In June 2017, I received a letter informing me that if I did not arrange to take the test within the next two weeks I would cease to be a member. It was not my wish, but neither was it my wish to participate in a legalistic exercise, which I think is unworthy of an organisation that claims counselling to be dependent upon an intensely personal relationship. I am sad to have been expelled since despite my ambivalence BACP has been good to me. But I will leave this profession as I started in it, with none of the pieces of paper that seem now to be of such importance. That matters less than that in my fifty years in counselling I have gained much, and in the grand scheme of things have given back a little on the way. I am grateful for that.

References

Agulnik, P., Holroyd, P. and Mandelbrote, B. (1976) The Isis Centre, a counselling service within the National Health Service, *British Medical Journal*, 2: 355–7.

Belbin, R.M. (1981) *Management Teams*. London: Heinemann.

Bell, E. (1996) *Counselling in Further and Higher Education*. Buckingham: Open University Press.

Bernfeld, S. (1962) On psychoanalytic training, *Psychoanalytic Quarterly*, 31: 453–82.

Brearley, J. (1995) *Counselling and Social Work*. Buckingham: Open University Press.

Couch, A. (1995) Anna Freud's adult psychoanalytical technique: a defence of classical analysis, *International Journal of Psychoanalysis*, 76: 151–71.

Counselling (1981) Rugby: British Association for Counselling.

Davies, D. and Neal, C. (eds.) (1996) *Pink Therapy*. Buckingham: Open University Press.

Davies, D. and Neal, C. (eds.) (2000) *Therapeutic Perspectives on Working with Lesbian, Gay and Bisexual Clients*. Buckingham: Open University Press.

Dryden, W. (1981) Some uses of audio-tape procedures in counselling: a personal view, *Counselling*, 36 (April): 14–17.

Dryden W. (ed.) (1992) *Hard-Earned Lessons from Counselling in Action*. London: Sage.

Dryden, W., Mearns, D. and Thorne, B. (2000) Counselling in the United Kingdom: past, present and future, *British Journal of Guidance and Counselling*, 28 (4): 467–84.

Ferrante, E. (2016) *Frantumaglia*. New York: Europa Editions.

Fowler, J. (1981) *Stages of Faith: The Psychology of Human Development and the Quest for Meaning*. New York: Harper & Row.

Fransella, F. (1996) Personal construct psychotherapy, in M. Jacobs (ed.) *Jitendra: Lost Connections*. Buckingham: Open University Press.

Fransella, F. and Dalton, P. (1990) *Personal Construct Counselling in Action*. London: Sage.

Freud, E. (ed.) (1970) *Letters of Sigmund Freud, 1873–1939*. London: Hogarth Press.

Halmos, P. (1965) *The Faith of the Counsellors*. London: Constable.

Jacobs, M. (1976) Naming and labelling, *Contact*, 54: 2–8.

Jacobs, M. (1980) *Optimism and Pessimism in the Theory and Practice of Therapy and Counselling*. Rugby: British Association for Counselling.

Jacobs, M. (1981a) Setting the record straight, *Counselling*, 36 (April): 10–13.

Jacobs, M. (ed.) (1981b) Proceedings of the BAC conference 'Counselling and the Unemployed Person'. Rugby: British Association for Counselling.

Jacobs, M. (1982) *Still Small Voice*. London: SPCK.

Jacobs, M. (1985a) *The Presenting Past*. London: Harper & Row.

Jacobs, M. (1985b) *Swift to Hear*. London: SPCK.

Jacobs, M. (1988) *Psychodynamic Counselling in Action*. London: Sage.

Jacobs, M. (1989) *Holding in Trust: The Use of Appraisal in Ministry*. London: SPCK.

Jacobs, M. (1990) A controlled explosion? – a decade of counselling training, *British Journal of Guidance and Counselling*, 18: 113–26.

Jacobs, M. (1991) *Insight and Experience*. Milton Keynes: Open University Press.

Jacobs, M. (1992a) *Sigmund Freud*. London: Sage.

Jacobs, M. (1992b) Michael Jacobs, in W. Dryden (ed.) *Hard-Earned Lessons from Counselling in Action*. London: Sage.

Jacobs, M. (1993a) *Living Illusions: A Psychology of Belief*. London: SPCK.

Jacobs, M. (1993b) The use of audio-tapes in counselling, in W. Dryden (ed.) *Questions and Answers on Counselling in Action*. London: Sage.

Jacobs, M. (ed.) (1995a) *In Search of a Therapist: Charlie – an Unwanted Child?* Buckingham: Open University Press.

Jacobs, M. (1995b) *D.W. Winnicott*. London: Sage.

Jacobs, M. (ed.) (1996a) *In Search of Supervision*. Buckingham: Open University Press.

Jacobs, M. (ed.) (1996b) *Jitendra: Lost Connections*. Buckingham: Open University Press.

Jacobs, M. (1998) *The Presenting Past*, 2nd edn. Buckingham: Open University Press.

Jacobs, M. (2000a) *Illusion: A Psychodynamic Interpretation of Thinking and Belief*. London: Whurr.

Jacobs, M. (2000b) Psychotherapy in the United Kingdom: past, present and future, *British Journal of Guidance and Counselling*, 28 (4): 451–66.

Jacobs, M. (2001) Standards of excellence, *Counselling and Psychotherapy Journal*, 12 (6): 16–17.

Jacobs, M. (2009a) *Our Desire of Unrest: Thinking about Therapy*. London: Karnac.

Jacobs, M. (2009b) A maturing professional approach, in *Our Desire of Unrest: Thinking about Therapy*. London: Karnac.

Jacobs, M. (2009c) Naming and labelling, in *Our Desire of Unrest: Thinking about Therapy*. London: Karnac.

Jacobs, M. (2009d) Optimism and pessimism, in *Our Desire of Unrest: Thinking about Therapy*. London: Karnac.

Jacobs, M. (2011) The aims of person therapy in training, *Psychodynamic Practice*, 17: 427–39.

Jacobs, M. and Walker, M. (2004) *Supervision: Questions and Answers for Counsellors and Therapists*. London: Whurr.

Khan, M.M.R. (1983) *Hidden Selves: Between Theory and Practice in Psychoanalysis*. London: Hogarth Press/Institute of Psychoanalysis.

Kohlberg, L. (1981) *The Philosophy of Moral Development*. San Francisco, CA: Harper & Row.

Kohut, H. (1971) *The Analysis of the Self*. Madison, CT: International Universities Press.

Lago, C. (1981) Establishing a counselling centre: a survey of counselling projects in their early days, *Counselling*, 36 (April): 18–25.

Lake, F. (1966) *Clinical Theology*. London: Darton, Longman & Todd. An abridged edition by Martin Yeomans followed some years later (London: Darton, Longman & Todd, 1986).

Langs, R. (1993) *Clinical Workbooks for Psychotherapy*. London: Karnac.

Lee, R.S. (1967) *Freud and Christianity*. London: Penguin Books.

Lee, R.S. (1973) *Principles of Pastoral Counselling*. London: SPCK.

Le Guin, U. (1971) *A Wizard of Earthsea.* London: Puffin Books.

Lowe, G. (1972) *The Growth of Personality.* Harmondsworth: Penguin Books.

Lyall, D. (1995) *Counselling in the Pastoral and Spiritual Context.* Buckingham: Open University Press.

MacDonald, E. (2014) *Skirting Heresy: The Life and Times of Margery Kempe.* Cincinnati, OH: Franciscan Media.

Mabey, K. and Sorensen, B. (1995) *Counselling for Young People.* Buckingham: Open University Press.

Murray, C. (2017) Accreditation and registration (Letter), *Therapy Today*, 28 (2): 17.

Neal, C. and Davies, D. (eds.) (2000) *Issues in Therapy with Lesbian, Gay, Bisexual and Transgender Clients.* Buckingham: Open University Press.

Newsome, A. (1980) Doctors and counsellors: collaboration or conflict?, *Bulletin of the Royal College of Psychiatrists*, July: 102–4.

Noonan, E. (1983) *Counselling Young People.* Hove: Brunner-Routledge.

Oldfield, S. (1983) *The Counselling Relationship: A Study of the Client's Experience.* London: Routledge & Kegan Paul.

Ratigan, B. (1981) Leicester counselling centre project: accreditation, supervision, training, *Counselling*, 36 (April): 5–9.

Rayner, E. (2005) *Human Development: An Introduction to the Psychodynamics of Growth, Maturity and Ageing*, 4th edn. London: Routledge.

Rowan, J. and Jacobs, M. (2002) *The Therapist's Use of Self.* Buckingham: Open University Press.

Ryle, A. (1990) *Cognitive-Analytic Therapy: Active Participation in Change.* Chichester: Wiley.

Salzberger-Wittenberg, I. (1970) *Psychoanalytic Insight and Relationships: A Kleinian Approach.* London: Routledge.

Samuels, A. and Jacobs M. (1995) *In Conversation with Andrew Samuels: Jung and the Post-Jungians.* Leicester: University of Leicester Audio-Visual Services.

Searles, H. (1986) *Collected Papers on Schizophrenia and Related Subjects.* London: Karnac.

Skynner, R. and Cleese, J. (1983) *Families and How to Survive Them.* London: Methuen.

Swainson, M. (1977) *Spirit of Counsel.* London: Neville Spearman.

Syme, G. (1994) *Counselling in Independent Practice*. Buckingham: Open University Press.

Tyndall, N. (1993) *Counselling in the Voluntary Sector*. Buckingham: Open University Press.

Walker, J. (1979) Student counselling services, in A. Wilkinson (ed.) *Student Health Practice*. Tunbridge Wells: Pitman Medical.

Walker, M. (1990) *Women in Therapy and Counselling: Out of the Shadows*. Milton Keynes: Open University Press.

Watts, A.G and Kidd, J. (2000) Guidance in the United Kingdom: past, present and future, *British Journal of Guidance and Counselling*, 28 (4): 485–502.

Index